Federal Budget Policy

Studies of Government Finance
TITLES PUBLISHED

Federal Budget Policy

DAVID J. OTT AND ATTIAT F. OTT

REVISED EDITION

Studies of Government Finance

THE BROOKINGS INSTITUTION

WASHINGTON, D. C.

Foreword

THIS VOLUME on federal budget policy is part of the Brookings series of Studies of Government Finance, a special program of research and education in taxation and government expenditures at the federal, state, and local levels, sponsored by the National Committee on Government Finance. It is a companion volume to two others in the series, James A. Maxwell's *Financing State and Local Governments* and Joseph A. Pechman's *Federal Tax Policy*. The purpose of these volumes is to present the accumulated knowledge of economists and others about government finances, so that public understanding of these areas may be advanced, the public's perception of issues may be sharpened, and factual and institutional materials may be readily at hand when the issues are publicly discussed.

The federal budget is important to every citizen. It is the basic planning document of the federal government, and at all times it exerts a significant influence on the state of the economy. This book describes and analyzes the history of federal expenditure and tax policy, the budget process itself, and the budget concepts that have been used to report federal fiscal activity. A special feature of the revised edition is a thorough description of the newest budget concept—the unified budget—which was recommended by the President's Commission on Budget Concepts in 1967 and adopted for presenting the fiscal year 1969 budget. The revised edition also includes a report on the impact of the planning-programming-budgeting system on the budget process.

This study and its revision were prepared jointly by David J. and

Attiat F. Ott, who are members of the economics faculty of Clark University. In preparing the original edition, the authors received help from many sources. They wish to express their appreciation for critical comments by Leonard S. Silk, Samuel M. Cohn, Otto Eckstein, Marshall A. Robinson, Naomi Sweeney, Charles B. Saunders, Jr., Carl Tiller, and Wilfred Lewis, Jr. Irene Lurie and Sheau-eng Lau acted as research assistants at different stages of the project, and Jane Brashares supervised the production of the final draft. The study, which was made under the direction of Joseph A. Pechman, Director of Economic Studies, was edited and indexed by Virginia C. Haaga. The revised edition was edited by Nancy C. Romoser and indexed by Helen B. Eisenhart. Evelyn P. Fisher carefully reviewed both editions for accuracy and consistency.

The revision was aided substantially by criticism, comments, and suggestions from William M. Capron, Rashi Fein, James A. Maxwell, and Naomi Sweeney. Richard Wagman served as research assistant.

The National Committee on Government Finance was established in 1960 by the trustees of the Brookings Institution to supervise a comprehensive program of studies on taxation and government expenditure. The program, sponsored by the National Committee, is supported with funds provided by the Ford Foundation.

The views expressed in this study are those of the authors and do not purport to represent the views of the National Committee on Government Finance, the staff members, officers, or trustees of the Brookings Institution, or the Ford Foundation.

Kermit Gordon
President

June 1969
Washington, D.C.

Studies of Government Finance

Studies of Government Finance is a special program of research and education in taxation and government expenditures at the federal, state, and local levels. This program, which is supported by a special grant from the Ford Foundation, was undertaken and supervised by the National Committee on Government Finance appointed by the trustees of the Brookings Institution.

MEMBERS OF THE ADVISORY COMMITTEE

Contents

Text Tables

Figures

Appendix Tables

CHAPTER I

Introduction

THIS BOOK IS ABOUT the federal budget, which amounts to one-fifth of total national output, or gross national product. Decisions regarding taxes and expenditures affect jobs, the "value of the dollar," the growth of the economy, and national defense. They bear on the questions of government versus private use of resources, federal versus state-local responsibility, and the viability of the private enterprise economy.

Those who make these critical decisions rely on staff specialists as well as on their own knowledge and experience. But the layman, who must ultimately judge the wisdom of the decisions, too often lacks the basis for informed judgment. To be informed about budget policy requires some familiarity with budget accounting concepts, the budget process, and the history of federal budget experience. To make informed judgments about federal spending and tax policy, knowledge of what the budget *should* do is also essential. This is true both for the President and his staff, who formulate federal budget policy, and for the congressman and the individual citizen, who must judge the President's fiscal program.

The purposes of this volume are (1) to explain, as far as possible in nontechnical language, the criteria that most economists would offer to guide decisions about federal spending and taxation, and (2) to provide institutional and descriptive material about the

1

federal budget, federal budgeting history, and how the budget is formulated to help the reader understand current budget policies.

The book begins with factual and descriptive background material. Chapter 2 explains the ways in which federal fiscal activity may be reported and the uses and limitations of each concept of the federal budget. Particular attention is given to the differences between the three most commonly used budgets in the past—the administrative, cash, and national income budgets—and to the unified budget recommended by the President's Commission on Budget Concepts in 1967 and adopted for the budget presented in January 1968. Chapter 3 tells how the federal budget is made, from the formulation and presentation of the President's budget through congressional consideration and approval, the actual disbursement of funds, and the audit of accounts. The impact of the so-called planning-programming-budgeting system (PPBS) on the budget process is given special emphasis. This chapter also summarizes past improvements in the budget process and suggests ways to make further improvements. Chapter 4 reviews the history of federal finances since 1790, including trends in federal expenditures relative to output, population, and prices and in the composition of federal expenditures. The trend in types of receipts is also discussed together with the record of deficits and surpluses.

The impact of budget policy on the nation's economy is discussed in Chapter 5. It explains how tax and expenditure decisions of the federal government affect output, employment, prices, economic growth, and the balance of payments and how budget policy together with monetary policy can help achieve certain economic goals related to output, employment, prices, growth, and the balance of payments. The practical problems involved in using the budget as an instrument to affect the economy are given special attention.

Chapter 6 deals with possible alternative budget programs. The virtues and problems of an annually balanced budget program are compared and contrasted with those of various other budget programs, such as the stabilizing budget proposal of the Committee for Economic Development and the Swedish budget proposals.

If the budget policy of the federal government requires running deficits and increasing the national debt, what will be the results? Is there a burden associated with the national debt? Will increases in the national debt lead to bankruptcy? These and other issues are taken up in Chapter 7.

The final chapter deals with criteria for judging federal spending —both the total amount and the amount for each function—apart from its impact on output, prices, and employment.

The reader should remember that not only is expenditure and tax policy important; it is also very controversial. The budget policy of an administration is often the leading domestic issue in national elections. This increases the need for the public to be informed on the facts and significance of budget decisions, but it also makes a completely objective study of budget policy more difficult, particularly since economists themselves disagree over some aspects of budget policy. The objectives of this volume are to present the views dominant among professional economists about budget policy and to indicate areas where disagreement exists.

CHAPTER II

The Federal Budget: Concepts and Uses

FEDERAL FISCAL ACTIVITY can be reported in a number of ways, and thus, in any discussion of federal budget policy, it must be made clear which budget concept is being used. In the past, different budget concepts have been emphasized in the President's budget in different years, with resulting confusion among the news media in their attempts to report on it, among congressmen in public statements and congressional debate, and certainly among the citizenry in discussing and evaluating federal budget policy. Charges of "gimmickry" have been leveled at the federal government from time to time when there have been switches in budget concepts.

In the midst of growing public concern over the citizen's ability to understand and evaluate federal budget policy in light of the various ways of reporting federal fiscal activity, President Johnson appointed the President's Commission on Budget Concepts in March 1967 to study the problems of presenting the federal budget and to make recommendations. The report of the commission (in October 1967) suggested a budget format that would reduce confusion but at the same time provide the necessary information for decisions on fiscal policy that affect the level of economic activity and for decisions on the allocation of resources among federal government

4

programs.[1] This budget concept was substantially adopted as the official format beginning with the fiscal year 1969 budget (presented in January 1968).

The new official budget will be discussed first, and then its relation to previously employed budget concepts—the administrative, consolidated cash, and national income accounts concepts—will be explained. A discussion of the so-called capital budget concept follows, and the chapter concludes with a short summary.

The Unified Federal Budget

The budget format recommended by the President's commission and now officially used (with a few exceptions noted below) is presented, for fiscal year 1967, in Table 1. (Supplementary, detailed tables are presented in Appendix A.) This budget has several special characteristics. First, it is comprehensive and integrated. It is comprehensive in that summary information is provided on all the complementary facets of the President's financial plan: (1) budget authority, both newly requested by the President or Congress and existing authority that will become available without any further action by Congress; (2) receipts, expenditures, and lending; (3) the total budget deficit or surplus; (4) how the deficit or surplus is to be financed; and (5) the implications of the budget for the amount of federal debt outstanding and the amount of federal debt held by the public. Included in expenditures and receipts are the trust funds (such as the old-age, survivors, disability, and health insurance trust funds—the social security trust funds) and those government-sponsored enterprises (such as the federal intermediate credit banks) which are partially owned by the federal government. Receipts and expenditures of the District of Columbia are excluded, however, and the district is treated as if it were a state or local government. In short, the budget provides a unified document on budget appropriations, receipts, expenditures, and net lending as part of the broad financial plan of the administration by relating these to means of financing the deficit (or use of the surplus). It does not concentrate on a single number, such as the budget surplus or deficit, but provides a unified set of summary data.

[1] *Report of the President's Commission on Budget Concepts* (Government Printing Office, 1967).

Table 1. Budget and Financial Plan of the United States Government, Fiscal Year 1967

(In billions of dollars)

Description	Amount
Budget Authority	
Requiring current action by Congress[a]	135.4
Becoming available without current action by Congress[a]	58.7
Deductions for interfund and intragovernmental transactions and applicable receipts[a]	−11.5
Total budget authority	182.6
Receipts, Expenditures, and Net Lending	
Expenditure account	
Receipts[b]	149.6
Expenditures (excluding net lending)[c]	153.2
Expenditure deficit	− 3.6
Loan account	
Loan disbursements	17.8
Loan repayments	−12.6
Net lending[c]	5.2
Total budget	
Receipts	149.6
Outlays (expenditures and net lending)	158.4
Budget deficit	− 8.8
Budget Financing[d]	
Borrowing from the public	3.6
Reduction of cash balances, and so on	5.3
Total budget financing	8.8

	1966 (actual)	1967
Outstanding debt at end of year		
Gross amount outstanding[d]	329.5	341.3
Amount held by the public[d]	265.6	269.2
Memorandum: Outstanding loans at end of year		
Direct loans (in loan account)		34.0
Guaranteed and insured loans		99.5

Source: U.S. Bureau of the Budget, *The Budget of the United States Government, Fiscal Year 1969* (1968), p. 51, hereinafter referred to as *Budget for Fiscal Year 1969.*
[a] For a breakdown of this amount, see Appendix Table A-15.
[b] For a breakdown of receipts by source, see Appendix Table A-2.
[c] For a breakdown of expenditures by function, see Appendix Table A-16.
[d] For a breakdown of the means of financing and the outstanding debt, see Appendix Table A-17.

A second special characteristic of the budget is that, at least for the time being, expenditures are counted when the government issues checks in payment of its obligations, and receipts are counted when checks are received from taxpayers and others. This is one of two major differences between the unified budget presented for 1969 and the budget recommended by the Commission on Budget Concepts.[2] The commission recommended putting all receipts and expenditures on an "accrual" basis—that is, counting expenditures when the government incurs a liability to pay for goods and services and counting receipts when the private sector incurs a liability to make payments to the federal government. The logic of accruing receipts and expenditures is that the economic impact of the budget presumably occurs as goods are produced for federal government use and as taxpayers incur a tax liability to the government. Lack of data prevented adoption of this recommendation in the 1969 budget, but it will presumably be used at some future time.

Third, the budget carefully distinguishes between loans and other expenditures and provides information on the surplus or deficit, both excluding and including loan outlays (as well as on gross disbursements and repayments of loans). This distinction is also based on the criterion of economic impact (net loan expenditures by the federal government have a different impact on the economy from purchases of goods or services or transfer payments, such as unemployment and social security benefits). When the federal government makes a loan, the recipient incurs a corresponding liability; his spending behavior is thus likely to be different from that of a recipient of social security benefits, for example, or a federal wage payment.

Fourth, although not implemented in the 1969 budget, the expenditure total will eventually include the subsidy element in federal loans.[3] What amounts to a subsidy arises because many federal loans are made at interest rates below Treasury borrowing costs, or, in some cases, carry a substantially higher risk of default. Thus, if the

[2] U.S. Bureau of the Budget, *The Budget of the United States Government, Fiscal Year 1969* (1968), p. 464. See the discussion by the commission of the problems of switching to an accrual basis in *Report of the President's Commission on Budget Concepts*, Chap. 4.

[3] The idea was accepted in principle by the Johnson administration, and efforts are currently being made to calculate this subsidy element and impute it to expenditures in future budgets. It should be noted that *all* nonrecourse loans such as those extended to farmers by the Commodity Credit Corporation are treated as expenditures, since they represent deferred commodity purchases.

federal government lends $100 for 40 years on an amortized basis at an interest rate of 2 percent but has to pay 5 percent to borrow the money from the public for the same term of years, the "loan" is worth only about $63, not $100. The $63 is the amount that *could* be lent at 5 percent for the same annual payments over the same period as the 2 percent loan. Thus the borrower receives an asset worth $100, but the government receives an asset in return worth only about $63. The $37 difference is conceptually equivalent to an ordinary transfer payment or subsidy and in future budgets will be counted as an expenditure at the time the loan is made. Putting this type of expenditure into the expenditure total will prevent the shifting of financing for programs from an expenditure to a loan basis, where the subsidy would not be imputed and total spending would appear lower. Other elements in the budget that are in effect subsidies are losses resulting from loans not repaid.

A fifth feature of the unified budget is the prominence given loans insured or guaranteed by the federal government. When the federal government insures or guarantees a private loan, the effect is conceptually similar to making the loan directly—the security guaranteed or insured becomes the equivalent of a Treasury issue; in both cases a government security (or the equivalent) is sold to one person and the funds are lent to another, and the same subsidy may be involved as with direct loans. However, in the case of guaranteed or insured loans there is the difference that no *actual* outlays are involved, so that budget receipts or expenditures cannot very well include an entry for such activities. The idea of giving prominence in the budget to the amount of guaranteed or insured loans outstanding is to provide some check to the incentive that might otherwise exist for shifting the financing of programs to this basis from a direct loan or expenditure basis, since such a shift would not otherwise show up in the budget.

Sixth, the unified budget treats federal government sales of participation certificates in loans which it continues to own as equivalent to issues of federal debt—a means of financing the deficit (or of using the surplus)—rather than as an offset (negative expenditure) to net federal lending.

Finally, budget receipts from government enterprise are treated as offsets to expenditures (negative expenditures) if the activity generating the receipts is "market oriented" as opposed to being essentially a "government activity," that is, one involving compulsion or regulation. Thus, the receipts of the Post Office from sales of stamps and fees are offset against its expenditures, and only the net deficit appears (as an expenditure item) in the budget. On the other hand, patent and copyright fees are counted as receipts and not netted out, since they result basically from a regulatory activity of the government.

We now turn to comparisons of the new budget with previously used or suggested budget concepts.

A Comparison of the Unified Budget and Other Budget Concepts

Three major budget concepts have been highlighted in budget presentations at one time or another in the past—the administrative, the consolidated cash, and the national income accounts (NIA) budgets. In comparison with the unified budget, the first mentioned—that is, the administrative budget—is distinctly less comprehensive, and the third, the NIA budget, does not relate complementary information on appropriations, means of financing, and outstanding federal debt and loans (direct and insured or guaranteed). In addition, there are significant differences in the definitions of "receipts, expenditures, and net lending" among all of these budget concepts.

The Administrative Budget

The administrative budget presents information on receipts and expenditures (including net lending) of "federally owned" funds. These are funds which technically *belong* to the federal government, in contrast to receipts and expenditures connected with trust funds (such as the old age, survivors, disability, and health insurance trust funds), for which the federal government acts technically only as trustee. The administrative budget therefore differs from the receipts, expenditures, and net lending section of the new budget primarily in coverage; it excludes trust fund receipts and expenditures whereas the official budget includes them. This alone makes it a deficient measure of federal fiscal activity, since there are some $37 billion of trust fund receipts and $31 billion of trust fund expenditures. In fact, the Commission on Budget Concepts recommended that "the President's budget presentation give no attention to a surplus or deficit calculated on the basis of the administrative budget."[4]

---

[4] *Report of the President's Commission on Budget Concepts,* p. 27.

The administrative budget differs from the new budget in several other respects: (1) Although it records expenditures almost entirely on a "checks-issued" basis, interest expense is recorded on an accrual basis (the timing of receipts and expenditures will differ even more if and when all receipts and expenditures in the unified budget are put on an accrual basis); (2) the administrative budget records receipts and expenditures only for wholly owned government enterprises, and receipts are netted against expenditures only when specific legislative authority provides for receipts to be applied to the financing of the activities which give rise to these receipts; (3) sales of participation certificates (commonly called PC's) in loans owned by the federal government are treated as an offset to net lending (negative expenditure) in the administrative budget, thus reducing total spending and the deficit below what it otherwise would be (the unified budget treats these as equivalent to sales of government securities); and (4) the administrative budget includes receipts from seignorage (the profit made on issuing coins) whereas the new budget excludes them.

Table 2 summarizes the adjustments necessary to reconcile the administrative budget deficit (or surplus) to the deficit (or surplus) in the new budget. (Since the additional netting of receipts of proprietary government-sponsored enterprises in the new budget involves subtraction from both receipts and expenditures, it does not appear in the adjustments.)

Table 2. Relation between the Unified Budget Deficit or Surplus and the Administrative Budget Deficit or Surplus, Fiscal Year 1967

(In billions of dollars)

Item	Amount
Administrative budget deficit (—) or surplus (+)	— 9.8
Adjustments needed to obtain unified budget deficit or surplus	
Trust fund receipts (adjusted for intragovernmental transactions)	37.0
Seignorage	— 0.8
Trust fund expenditures (adjusted for intragovernmental transactions)	—30.9
Expenditures of government-sponsored enterprises with private ownership	— 0.1
Net sales of participation certificates	— 3.5
Timing: debt issued in lieu of checks for international institutions	— 0.2
Other adjustments	— 0.4
Unified budget deficit (—) or surplus (+)	— 8.8

Source: *Budget for Fiscal Year 1969*, p. 466. Details may not add to total because of rounding.

The Consolidated Cash Budget

The consolidated cash statement is a measure of transactions between the federal government and the public; it is "consolidated" in the sense that both federal funds and trust funds are included and "cash" in the sense that receipts and payments are on a checks-*paid* basis as distinguished from the checks-*issued* basis of the administrative budget. Since trust funds are included in the cash budget, differences in receipts and expenditures (including net lending) between this budget and the unified budget (Table 3) are not nearly as large as between the administrative and unified budgets.

Table 3. Relation between Unified Budget Totals and Consolidated Cash Budget Totals, Fiscal Year 1967

(In billions of dollars)

Item	Amount
Cash budget receipts	153.6
Adjustments needed to obtain unified budget receipts	
Coverage: D.C. municipal funds	−0.3
Netting of proprietary receipts not netted in cash budget	−4.9
Federal employee retirement contributions	1.2
Employer payments to government for social security	−0.5
Social security annuitants' payments for supplementary medical insurance	0.5
Total receipts in unified budget	149.6
Cash budget expenditures and net lending	155.1
Adjustments needed to obtain unified budget outlays	
Coverage: D.C. municipal funds	−0.3
Netting of proprietary receipts	−4.9
Federal employee retirement contributions	1.2
Exclusion of privately owned government-sponsored institutions	3.9
Timing adjustments (conversion from a checks-issued to a checks-paid basis)	1.1
Net sales of participation certificates	2.6
Other adjustments	−0.2
Total unified budget outlays	158.4

Source: *Budget for Fiscal Year 1969*, p. 466. Details may not add to totals because of rounding.

The major differences introduced by the unified budget, as compared with the cash budget, are (1) reductions in both receipts and expenditures as a result of treating certain enterprise-type receipts on a net rather than a gross basis under the "market-oriented" criterion; (2) additions to both receipts and expenditures of federal employee retirement contributions; (3) an increase in expenditures resulting from treating PC's as a means of financing rather than as negative expenditures; (4) exclusion of the transactions of two privately owned government-sponsored enterprises (federal land banks and federal home loan banks); and (5) timing adjustments to convert expenditures from a "checks-paid" to a "checks-issued" basis.

The Federal Sector of the National Income Accounts

The federal sector of the national income accounts, or the "national income accounts budget" as it is often called, corresponds in concept to the system followed in the national income accounts, a system of dual-entry accounts used by the Department of Commerce to estimate the current productive activity of residents of the United States. On the one hand, the accounts show the market values of the currently produced output of goods and services, classified by type of expenditure: consumer expenditures, gross private expenditures on equipment, new construction, and inventories, federal, state, and local government purchases of goods and services, and net exports. The total of these items is called gross national product (GNP). On the other hand, the accounts measure and classify the stream of income generated in the process of producing GNP: wages and salaries, professional income, rental income, corporate profits, interest, and others.

The federal sector of the national income accounts differs from receipts and outlays in the unified budget principally in three respects: (1) the timing of receipts and expenditures is different; (2) net lending (as well as some lending and asset exchanges not in the loan account of the unified budget) is excluded from NIA expenditures; and (3) *government* contributions to the civil service and foreign service retirement plans are treated as "gross" (added to receipts and expenditures) in the NIA rather than netted out as intragovernmental transactions, as in the unified budget.

The timing differences in recording receipts and outlays reflect the fact that the unified budget at present counts receipts when the cash is collected and most expenditures when checks are issued; in the NIA budget, on the other hand, receipts (except for nonwithheld personal taxes) are reported on an accrual basis (when income is earned or when a liability to pay the federal government is incurred), but expenditures are reported in several ways—on an accrual basis for construction and interest outlays, on a "delivery" basis for other goods purchases, and on a checks-issued basis for grants-in-aid, subsidies, and transfer payments. An adjustment must thus be made in order to reconcile the differences in the timing of receipts and expenditures in the two budgets.

Net lending is excluded from NIA outlays because it represents an exchange of one asset for another, *not* an expenditure for currently produced goods and services. In fact, the NIA budget excludes more net lending than the amount in the loan account of the unified budget. The unified budget loan account includes only those domestic loan transactions in which definite requirements for full repayment are specified, plus all foreign loans made on commercial terms. The NIA budget excludes not only these loans but such others as foreign loans under the Agency for International Development (AID) and tobacco and foreign loans of the Commodity Credit

Table 4. Relation between Unified Budget Totals and National Income Accounts Budget Totals, Fiscal Year 1967

(In billions of dollars)

Item	Amount
NIA receipts	147.6
Adjustments needed to obtain unified budget receipts	
Employer share of employee retirement (grossing)	−1.7
Other netting and grossing	−1.1
Adjustment to cash-collected basis	4.8
Other	ᵃ
Receipts in unified budget	149.6
Expenditures in NIA budget	155.1
Adjustments needed to obtain unified budget expenditures	
Net lending in unified budget	5.2
Other lending excluded from NIA but not from unified budget loan account	1.4
Employer share of employee retirement (grossing)	−1.7
Other netting and grossing	−1.1
Dollar expenditures to finance agricultural exports	0.8
Timing adjustment for defense purchases	0.4
Other adjustments (asset transactions, timing, expenditure of foreign currency)	−1.6
Expenditures and net lending in unified budget	158.5

Source: *Budget for Fiscal Year 1969*, pp. 51, 477–80. Details may not add to totals because of rounding.
ᵃ Less than $50 million.

FIGURE 1. Federal Deficits and Surpluses under Four Budget Concepts for Fiscal Years 1948–67

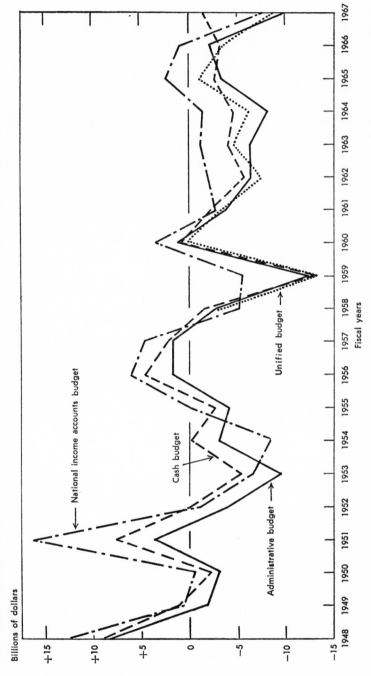

Billions of dollars

Fiscal years

Sources: U.S. Bureau of the Budget, *The Budget of the United States Government, Fiscal Year 1968* (1967), pp. 452–53; and *The Budget of the United States Government, Fiscal Year 1969* (1968), pp. 466, 538, and 542. These documents are hereinafter cited as *Budget for Fiscal Year 1968* or *1969*.

Corporation (CCC). Also excluded are exchanges of assets such as dollar outlays by the CCC to acquire foreign currencies to pay for agricultural exports. CCC nonrecourse loans, however, are included in the NIA budget as purchases of goods and services.

Both receipts and outlays in the NIA budget are increased by the amount of government contributions to its employee retirement plans because these amounts are counted as part of the compensation of employees who in turn pay it back to the government as their retirement contribution. Table 4 shows the overall relation between receipts and outlays of the unified budget and the NIA budget.

The major differences between the four budget concepts are summarized in Table 5, and Figure 1 shows how these differences affect each budget concept's deficit or surplus for fiscal years 1948–67.

The Capital, or Divided, Budget

From time to time a proposal has been made that the federal government should adopt still another method in presenting its budget—the so-called capital budget.[5] The basic idea of the divided budget is separation of the budget into two parts—the "current" and "capital" accounts. The rationale for this format is that it is more "businesslike" in its approach to federal finance (and that it is the format typically used at the state-local level). Since business firms do not count purchases of durable assets as a cost *when they are purchased* but only as they are depreciated, why should federal expenditures include purchases of assets as an expenditure (cost)? Why not follow business practices and count as current expenditures only purchases of nondurable goods (and services), transfer payments, interest, grants-in-aid to state and local governments, and *depreciation of the government's stock of assets?*

The general format of the divided budget is shown in Table 6 with some hypothetical dollar entries. The current account shows all expenditures except purchases of assets by the government and all

[5] A good source for a summary of the arguments for and against a divided budget for the U.S. government is Maynard S. Comiez, *A Capital Budget Statement for the U.S. Government* (Brookings Institution, 1966). He also presents the results of converting the U.S. budget to a divided budget; these findings will be discussed later in this section.

Table 5. Major Differences among Four Budget Concepts

| Item | Unified budget | | Adminis-trative budget | Consolidated cash budget | National income accounts budget |
	Receipt-expenditure account	Total			
Coverage					
Treatment of trust funds	Included	Included	Excluded	Included	Included
Treatment of District of Columbia	Excluded	Excluded	Excluded	Included	Excluded
Government-sponsored enterprises	Included, except two privately owned	Included, except two privately owned	Excluded	Included	Included, except two privately owned
Timing					
Receipts	Collections[a]	Collections[a]	Collections	Collections	Accrued
Expenditures					
Interest	Checks issued[a]	Checks issued[a]	Accrued	Checks paid	Accrued
Defense	Checks issued[a]	Checks issued[a]	Checks issued	Checks paid	Delivery
Other	Checks issued[a]	Checks issued[a]	Checks issued	Checks paid	Checks issued
Federal lending					
Domestic loans	Excluded	Included	Included	Included	Excluded
Foreign loans	Included	Included	Included	Included	Excluded
Loan subsidy imputation	Excluded[b]	Excluded[b]	Excluded	Excluded	Excluded
Criterion for netting receipts	Character of enterprise	Character of enterprise	Legal funding basis	Legal funding basis	Legal funding basis
Treatment of participation certificates	Means of finance	Means of finance	Negative expenditure	Negative expenditure	Means of finance

Source: President's Commission on Budget Concepts, *Staff Papers and Other Materials Reviewed by the President's Commission* (1967).

[a] To be put on an accrual basis at a later date, based on Commission on Budget Concepts recommendation.

[b] To be included at a later date, based on Commission on Budget Concepts recommendation.

Table 6. An Illustration of a Divided Budget

(Hypothetical dollar amounts)

Expenditures		Receipts	
Current account			
Purchases of current goods		Corporate tax receipts	80
and services	130	Personal income tax	
Transfer payments	50	receipts	120
Grants-in-aid to state and		Excise tax receipts	10
local governments	40	Other tax and nontax	
Depreciation on government		receipts	30
assets	40		
	—		—
Total	260	Total	240
Surplus or deficit on current account — 20			
Capital account			
Purchases of government		Sales of government assets	10
assets	100	Transfer from current account	
		for depreciation	40
	—		—
Total	100	Total	50
Surplus or deficit on capital account — 50			
Overall budget surplus (+) or deficit (—) —70			

receipts except sales of government assets or government borrowing. The capital account shows purchases of government assets as expenditures and sales of government assets and funds transferred from the current account to cover depreciation as receipts.

The budget presented this way shows a deficit of 70—20 in the current account and 50 in the capital account. The rationale for splitting the overall deficit into two parts is that the part of the deficit used to finance purchases of assets (50) is different—the excess of expenditures over receipts used to acquire capital assets and covered by borrowing does not change the government's net asset position since the new debt is matched by a new government asset. A deficit in the current account is thus the "true" deficit in the sense that it does reduce the net assets of the government (or increase its net liabilities).

Several arguments have been advanced for a divided budget as opposed to a unified, cash, or NIA budget. One of these is that it would provide a better summary of the cost of government activities since the costs of government capital assets would be allocated over time by means of the depreciation entry in the current account.

It is sometimes also argued that a divided budget would provide information on capital accumulation in the government sector not currently reflected in the NIA measure of investment outlays in the economy as a whole. However, formal use of a divided budget is not essential to measure the accumulation of assets by the government; it could be provided by a special analysis within a unified budget.

To many, a major advantage of capital budgeting is that it would enhance the political acceptability of capital expenditures and borrowing by the government. It seems to offer the chance simultaneously to reduce the size of the government's deficit while allowing large-scale borrowing; it provides a rationale for deficit financing. Tax requirements would likely be assessed mainly by reference to the current account portion of the budget; and since expenditures in the capital account portion could be covered largely by borrowing, they would escape somewhat the usual political checks.[6]

In a study prepared for the Brookings Institution, Maynard Comiez converted the U.S. administrative and cash budget statements for fiscal years 1955–63 to a divided budget format, using a variety of assumptions about where to draw the line between capital and current outlays, techniques for determining depreciation rates, and so forth.[7] Table 7 shows his main findings for the two models of divided budgets he considered to be the most meaningful (II and VII): although conversion to a divided budget *would* reduce the deficit (increase the surplus) in the current account, as compared with the deficit (or surplus) in the administrative or cash budget, it would not have turned budget deficits into surpluses in any year.

[6] Note, however, that depreciation charges on government assets appear as an expenditure in the current account. If the rate of purchase of government assets were held constant over time, the depreciation charge would eventually equal new outlays for depreciable assets, and the size of the current account deficit would be the same as in a unified budget. The current account of a divided budget will show smaller deficits than a cash budget when capital outlays are rising over a period and larger deficits when capital outlays are falling over a period. The difference between the deficits or surpluses in the current account of a divided budget and in a unified budget will be smaller the higher the depreciation rate on government assets; the shorter the useful lives of government assets, the faster they will be depreciated and show up as a charge in the current account.

[7] Comiez, *A Capital Budget Statement for the U.S. Government,* esp. pp. 40–48, 61–77, 106–12.

Table 7. Comparison of the Current Account Surplus (or Deficit) under Two Divided Budget Models with the Surplus (or Deficit) in the Administrative and Cash Budgets, Fiscal Years 1955–63

(In millions of dollars)

Year	Divided budget surplus (+) or deficit (−) on current account, Model II	Administrative budget surplus (+) or deficit (−)	Divided budget surplus (+) or deficit (−) on current account, Model VII	Cash budget surplus (+) or deficit (−)
1955	−1,849	−4,180	− 408	−2,702
1956	3,409	1,626	6,297	4,542
1957	1,489	1,596	2,243	2,099
1958	−1,555	−2,819	− 610	−1,580
1959	−6,692	−12,427	−7,124	−13,092
1960	2,588	1,224	2,539	750
1961	−2,121	−3,856	− 486	−2,300
1962	−4,102	−6,378	−3,016	−5,797
1963	−3,389	−6,266	−1,446	−4,012

Source: Maynard S. Comiez, *A Capital Budget Statement for the U.S. Government* (Brookings Institution, 1966), p. 139.

It is sometimes asserted that a divided budget provides a workable means of regulating the amount of government borrowing—taxes can be set to cover expenditures in the current account and borrowing can be set to cover the cost of capital outlays *not* covered by the depreciation transfer from the current account and sales of assets. In short, borrowing is used to cover *net* capital outlays (capital outlays *minus* depreciation) of the government. With this budget policy, taxes need not be changed as often since they are not used to finance capital outlays; the government can defer the *final* allocation among the public of the burden of its capital outlays (since taxes are levied to pay the depreciation charges as they occur); and a more rational division of national output is provided between consumption and investment (loan finance is likely to reduce private investment more than tax finance, and thus government investment is more likely to be a substitute for private investment under the rule of borrowing for net government investment).

This argument for a capital budget is difficult to take too seriously. Decisions in regard to taxes and borrowing must be made with reference to the economic impact of the *total* budget, that is, taxes should be set to achieve the desired impact on output, prices, and the balance of payments, given the *total* amount of government outlays. A policy which ties borrowing to government net investment and taxes to current outlays would only by sheer coincidence produce the desired effect on aggregate demand, output, prices, and the balance of payments.

The major criticism of the divided, or capital, budget is that it would distort priorities in government programs. Projects qualifying for the capital account would have an advantage in the annual budgetary competition over those qualifying only for the ordinary budget, since the outlays in one case would show up immediately in the current account whereas in the other case they would appear only over time as the asset was depreciated. As former Budget Director Kermit Gordon put it:

This would introduce a bias in favor of investment in bricks and concrete as against investment in people and knowledge; yet if one were looking in the present budget for examples of unproductive investment, one's search would be rewarded more quickly in the former area than in the latter.[8]

Futhermore, there are a host of unresolved conceptual issues in implementing a capital budget. For example, should the capital budget show gross or net capital outlays? Should only federally owned assets be included or should assets financed by the federal government but owned by others (such as the interstate highway system) also be included? On the receipts side, there are also a number of issues. Should, for example, receipts from death taxes and capital levies be allocated to the capital budget in order to maintain society's total capital stock (on the presumption that these levies reduce private capital formation more than taxes on current income)? This is, of course, a question that can be answered empirically, but there is no conclusive evidence yet to support or refute the presumption behind it.

These are but a few of the difficult questions that must be answered before the actual implementation of a capital budget and

[8] Kermit Gordon, "Reflections on Spending," *Public Policy,* Vol. 15 (1966), (Brookings Reprint 125), pp. 8–9. See pp. 7–9 for a good discussion of the arguments against capital budgeting at the federal level.

that led the President's Commission on Budget Concepts to reject the idea for the U.S. government.[9]

Summary

This chapter has emphasized the differences between the unified budget adopted in 1967 and other budget concepts that have received attention in budget presentations or in discussions of budget policy in recent and past periods. The great virtues of the unified budget are its comprehensiveness, consistency, and flexibility of use. It is comprehensive in providing a set of complementary sections which not only treat the budget as narrowly defined—receipts, expenditures, and net lending—but provide interlocking data on the "before and after"—appropriations, means of financing, and loans and loan guarantees outstanding. It is consistent in its treatment of the conceptual problems summarized in Table 5—coverage, timing, loans, loan subsidies, netting of receipts, and treatment of participation certificates—in each case a carefully considered criterion is used (for example the "market-oriented" or "governmental" character of a government enterprise) to decide the treatment of each receipt or expenditure account. The official budget is flexible in that it provides in one place the budget information needed for various purposes, such as assessing the economic impact of the budget, gauging the size of the federal government, and measuring the government's impact in financial markets.

In contrast, none of the alternative budget concepts—the administrative, cash, or national income accounts budget—has all of these advantages. Either there are inconsistencies in the treatment of receipt or expenditure items or certain information is missing. The capital budget concept has some appeal conceptually, but it is likely to be misleading to an unsophisticated public and it presents many problems of implementation. Throughout our discussion in the chapters that follow, the budget referred to will be the unified budget, unless specified otherwise.

[9] *Report of the President's Commission on Budget Concepts,* pp. 33–34.

CHAPTER III

The Budget Process

CRUCIAL TO ANY discussion of budget policy—the setting of levels and composition of taxes and expenditures to achieve certain goals —is a knowledge of the administrative and political process through which expenditures and taxes are, in fact, determined. This chapter describes the process at the federal level and also indicates briefly the forces and individuals involved in making the many difficult decisions that go into the final budget.

Although budgeting is a continuing process, the term "budget cycle" is often used to emphasize its periodicity. There are clearly defined phases of budgeting in most budgetary systems. At the federal level in the United States, four phases can be identified: (1) executive preparation and submission, (2) legislative authorization and appropriation, (3) execution, and (4) audit.

Executive Preparation and Submission

Every year the executive branch of the federal government prepares the budget, which in January is submitted to the Congress by the President with his budget message. This budget is for the fiscal year beginning on the first of July following transmittal of the budget message. However, preparation of the budget begins long before January. Figure 2 shows the approximate time sequence of, and participants in, each stage of budget preparation by the executive branch. The timing suggested is only approximate since it may vary under different pressures or in different departments. Nevertheless, the chart does indicate the lead time required to prepare the executive's budget.

Figure 2 illustrates a basic characteristic of budgeting in the executive branch—the two-way flow of decisions, up from the departments and agencies and then back down from the Bureau of the Budget and the President.[1] The individual organizational units in the departments and agencies make early plans for their programs and expenditures, which are consolidated and reviewed by the budget offices in each agency. The budget offices provide the agency with information when, in May, June, and July, programs for the coming year are discussed with the Bureau of the Budget. The bureau then can advise the President about preliminary agency and department plans and goals. This information, together with projections of the economic outlook and revenue estimates from the Treasury, the Bureau of the Budget, and the Council of Economic Advisers (in June, July, or August), gives the President and his advisers the basis for tentative overall budget policy decisions—about total expenditures, revenues, and programs. Guidelines reflecting these policy decisions then flow back down through the Bureau of the Budget to the departments and agencies in the form of planning figures to guide the preparation of their eventual budget submissions in the fall. They must then either modify their programs to fit the guidelines or appeal to the Bureau of the Budget and possibly even to the executive for a reversal of a decision affecting their budgets.

Three facets of the budget-making process are apparent in Figure 2: (1) the program-issue orientation of most of the budget process through late September; (2) the fiscal policy decisions about total expenditures and taxes that become crucial in the late summer and early fall of each year; and (3) the meshing of these two facets

[1] It should be noted that the budget of the Department of Defense is handled somewhat differently from those of other agencies. The Bureau of the Budget participates with the financial officers of the Defense Department in a review of the requests of the various services for budgetary allowances, but its role here is not quite the same as with other agencies. It acts more as an adviser to the Secretary of Defense than as an arbiter; more decisions in this agency must be left for presidential action. In addition, final Defense budgetary decisions are made later than those of other agencies; many of the crucial ones are held until late December.

FIGURE 2. Formulation of the Executive Budget

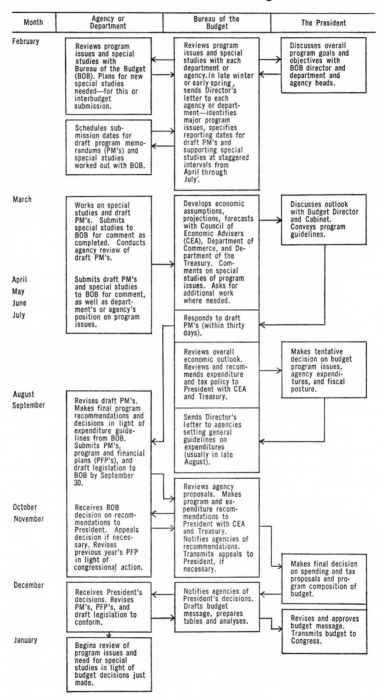

Month	Agency or Department	Bureau of the Budget	The President
February	Reviews program issues and special studies with Bureau of the Budget (BOB). Plans for new special studies needed—for this or interbudget submission. Schedules submission dates for draft program memorandums (PM's) and special studies worked out with BOB.	Reviews program issues and special studies with each department or agency. In late winter or early spring, sends Director's letter to each agency or department—identifies major program issues, specifies reporting dates for draft PM's and supporting special studies at staggered intervals from April through July.	Discusses overall program goals and objectives with BOB director and department and agency heads.
March	Works on special studies and draft PM's. Submits special studies to BOB for comment as completed. Conducts agency review of draft PM's.	Develops economic assumptions, projections, forecasts with Council of Economic Advisers (CEA), Department of Commerce, and Department of the Treasury. Comments on special studies of program issues. Asks for additional work where needed.	Discusses outlook with Budget Director and Cabinet. Conveys program guidelines.
April May June July	Submits draft PM's and special studies to BOB for comment, as well as department's or agency's position on program issues.	Responds to draft PM's (within thirty days). Reviews overall economic outlook. Reviews and recommends expenditure and tax policy to President with CEA and Treasury.	Makes tentative decision on budget program issues, agency expenditures, and fiscal posture.
August September	Revises draft PM's. Makes final program recommendations and decisions in light of expenditure guidelines from BOB. Submits PM's, program and financial plans (PFP's), and draft legislation to BOB by September 30.	Sends Director's letter to agencies setting general guidelines on expenditures (usually in late August).	
October November	Receives BOB decision on recommendations to President. Appeals decision if necessary. Revises previous year's PFP in light of congressional action.	Reviews agency proposals. Makes program and expenditure recommendations to President with CEA and Treasury. Notifies agencies of recommendations. Transmits appeals to President, if necessary.	Makes final decision on spending and tax proposals and program composition of budget.
December	Receives President's decisions. Revises PM's, PFP's, and draft legislation to conform.	Notifies agencies of President's decisions. Drafts budget message, prepares tables and analyses.	Revises and approves budget message. Transmits budget to Congress.
January	Begins review of program issues and need for special studies in light of budget decisions just made.		

of budget formulation in the final budget decisions in November and December.

PPBS and Program-Orientation in the Budget Process

The orientation of executive budgeting toward program issues is a relatively new phenomenon. It began in an informal way under President Kennedy and, in August 1965, was formally introduced by President Johnson in the form of an integrated planning-programming-budgeting system (PPBS) in the executive branch, to be used initially during late 1965 and 1966 in the preparation of the budget that would be submitted in January 1967 (the fiscal year 1968 budget) and to be developed further thereafter. The adoption of PPBS has already had a considerable impact on the budget process (as Figure 2 shows) and will likely have an even greater effect in the longer run.

Under PPBS budgeting, the focus is on the *uses* of federal expenditures—on the *output* provided for—rather than on dollar amounts allocated by agency or department. The aim of PPBS is to specify (and where possible to quantify) the objectives, or "output," of federal spending programs and then to minimize the cost of achieving these objectives or to ascertain whether program benefits exceed costs. To do so requires the *systematic use of analysis* in connection with budget formulation and program development and evaluation (the "planning" in PPBS).

The hallmarks of PPBS, then, are (1) specification of the objectives to be achieved through federal spending, (2) investigation of alternative means of achieving the objectives, (3) minimization of the costs or comparison of costs and benefits (when the benefits can be quantified), and perhaps most important, (4) systematic use of analysis throughout the process. Specifying the objectives, or output, of the budget really begins with the President, according to a former Budget Bureau director, Kermit Gordon:

. . . for the budget is his plan, and the implied priorities are his priorities. . . . The budget is the President's budget, in a real as well as in a formal sense.[2]

Departments or agencies may vary in the extent to which they

---

[2] Kermit Gordon, "Reflections on Spending," *Public Policy,* Vol. 15 (1966) (Brookings Reprint 125), p. 11.

specify goals consistent with the "presidential perspective," as Gordon characterizes it.[3] Under PPBS, however, when department or agency objectives are inconsistent with the President's priorities, it is immediately obvious. The first step under PPBS is to reorganize the budget structures of departments and agencies, so that their activities are grouped under a relatively small number (five to ten) of major "program packages." These in turn are divided into subordinate categories, which are made up of a large number of "program elements." The next step is to develop indices or measures to indicate the level of accomplishment under each program (the output), how much the various program elements contribute to "output" under the program, and the cost of the elements. This step leads directly to the second and third features of PPBS—analysis of the alternative means of achieving program objectives, and choice of the least-cost combination of program elements to achieve a given output.

Three department or agency documents are critical in the budget process under PPBS: (1) the program memorandum (PM), (2) the program and financial plan (PFP), and (3) special analytic studies. The program memorandum provides an explicit statement of the objectives, goals, and strategy (program) of the agency; it shows the agency's choices of programs and program elements. In addition, it summarizes the analytic studies that have led to the choices and identifies major policy issues relating to each program.[4]

The program and financial plan is basically designed to present the future implications of current decisions. It presents pertinent data on output and costs for a five-year period (the current fiscal year plus at least four future fiscal years) for each program element, *based on current decisions*. It is *not* a projection of future activities and spending by the agency, since decisions may be made to enlarge, reduce, or eliminate programs in the future, but only an attempt to show the agency, the Budget Bureau, and the President the implications, in terms of outputs and costs, of current program decisions.

The special analytic studies, which are prepared by agency PPB specialists, provide the underlying analysis on which choices of pro-

---

[3] *Ibid.*, p. 15.
[4] Since PPBS is relatively new, many decisions cannot be made on the basis of analytic studies, and in such cases only a brief statement of reasons for the choice is required.

grams and program elements are based. These may include rather elaborate efforts to compare costs and benefits of various programs, simply to define the goals and output of a program, or to analyze the "cost-effectiveness" of alternative programs (to see which achieves a given goal at least cost to the government).[5]

Since PPBS is relatively new, it is too early to evaluate and measure the results against the initial hopes and expectations. There is considerable variation in the extent to which the departments and agencies have embraced the system; some have shown considerable enthusiasm and have already gone far in developing program and program element categories and in undertaking the necessary analytic studies. Others have not been very responsive and will move in this direction only with considerable prodding from the Bureau of the Budget (and perhaps the President). However, the point is that at least formally the budget process is being focused on the *objectives* of federal programs and there is no longer a preoccupation with *inputs*. In addition, increasing emphasis is being placed on systematic program analysis and evaluation.

Budget Review: The Director's Letter

The budget process from early February through the summer is referred to as the "budget preview." The first step in this part of the budget process is the development of a director's letter.[6]

During February, departments and agencies confer with the Bureau of the Budget on the coming budget. The most important aspect of this early consultation is to identify, for each department or agency, a set of "program issues"—decisions that must be made regarding the scope and size of the agency's programs and program elements. These partly reflect program issues left over from the previous year's budget process; new issues are also raised.

The program issues for each agency are the product of negotiations between the BOB and the agency, often at the highest levels. The director of the Budget Bureau discusses in general terms program priorities with the President and his White House staff; these

[5] A more detailed discussion of the uses of cost-benefit and cost-effectiveness analysis is presented in Chapter 8. The interest here is in how these are reflected in the budget process.

[6] The timetable and specific steps in the budget process reflected in this discussion are subject to adjustment and modification. PPBS is a new system and is undergoing change as experience is gained.

are reflected in his and his staff's discussions with the departments and agencies. At this early stage, then, the program orientation of the budget process already reflects, in a broad sense, the presidential perspective.

The discussions and decisions on program issues lead rather naturally to simultaneous consideration of the special analytic studies needed from each agency. Since these studies often cannot be geared to an annual budget cycle, plans will be laid for studies over two- or three-year periods, as well as for interim studies to provide limited information for decision making in the current year.

By late winter or early spring, the Budget director sends a letter to each department or agency head. This letter formalizes the agreements reached on program issues and analytic studies for each agency. It also specifies the dates each agency is to submit a draft program memorandum, together with analytic studies, to the Budget Bureau. The reporting dates are scheduled at staggered intervals from April through the summer.

Agency Budget Preview Activities

After the director's letter has gone out, the budget process centers in the agencies and departments. The activities there focus on (1) initiation and completion of analytic studies needed to reach decisions on the program issues identified in the director's letter, (2) intra-agency budget reviews for which the analytic studies are used to make program decisions, and (3) preparation of draft PM's, PFP's, legislation, and analytic studies for submission to the Budget Bureau.

All federal agencies and departments have budget offices and officers. The organization of the offices may vary, but generally the budget officer serves as a member of the department or agency staff. Since the initiation of PPBS, all agencies and departments also have staffs or specialists in PPBS analysis, both at the top of the agency or department and down in the "line," or operating, agencies. In fiscal year 1968, some 685 PPBS professionals were located in 21 agencies or departments (not including the Department of Defense). About half represented new additions to staffs; the other half were previous employees redesignated or converted to PPBS analysis.[7]

---

[7] Information from the Bureau of the Budget. In contrast, only some 15–20 members of the Budget Bureau staff are PPBS specialists. This illustrates a point

These specialists undertake the analytic studies suggested by the director's letter. The studies are done at the operating level in many agencies and reviewed by other specialists at the agency or department level. In other agencies, much of the analytic work has thus far been centered in the agency or department staff.

Through the agency budgeting office and professional staffs flows the information on programs and costs needed by the administrator to decide on program issues raised in the director's letter as well as programs and costs not at issue in the current year's budget. Often it is impossible to conduct the needed analysis in the time provided, and program issues may have to be decided on rather diverse grounds, ranging from the political pressures that may be swirling around a program to the administrator's intuitive judgment. Many agency or department programs and much of their budgets may not be included in the program issues raised in the director's letter. Every program cannot be studied carefully every year, and some may coast along on their own impetus. Further, a large segment of budget expenditures is virtually outside the budget process and will not often be reflected in program issues. For the last few years, for example, such items as interest on the public debt, veterans' pensions, and agricultural price supports have accounted for over 60 percent of total nondefense budget expenses and for over 25 percent of total budget expenditures. The levels of expenditure for these items are determined by provisions written into legislation authorizing the programs and by other factors not readily subject to annual budgetary control. They are, however, subject to review, and occasionally, legislation is proposed to change them. The crucial budget decisions, then, relate primarily to programs subject to budgetary control and take the form of an evaluation of relatively small increases in costs and activities.

The focus of the budget preview process on program issues and the use of the analytical paraphernalia of PPBS should not obscure the fact that budget making is and always will be a *political* process, and the politics of budget making are important in several ways at the agency level. Agencies and their "line people" are expected to be advocates of increased appropriations. It is generally accepted as

worth noting, namely, PPBS is not a technique for building up the Budget Bureau's powers relative to the agencies but for giving the agencies devices to evaluate their own activities better.

natural and inevitable by Congress and the Budget Bureau that agency budget offices will have a strong interest in justifying their program decisions and appropriation requests. After all, they are expected to believe in their work and be enthusiastic about it. In fact, Congress and the Bureau of the Budget would find their task much more difficult if the agencies refused to play the role of advocate; as advocates the agencies supply information crucial to congressional and Budget Bureau decisions—information Congress and the bureau would otherwise have to obtain for themselves.

On the other hand, agencies or departments rarely ask for all they feel they could use. If they did, the Bureau of the Budget or Congress would probably make substantial cuts; to have proposals cut sharply every year would set an unfortunate precedent, and in any case, some cuts are inevitable in an agency budget. As guardians of the public purse, the Budget Bureau and Congress are expected to be more economy-minded than agency heads, who are responsible for the execution rather than the financing of specific programs. Moreover, the bureau has the task of weighing budget requests across the whole range of federal activity—it must make recommendations to the President concerning the choices open to him.

So in making decisions on programs and expenditures, agencies cannot, for strategic reasons, aim too high or too low. Their decision making will reflect seeking out and receiving clues and hints from the executive branch, Congress, clientele groups, and their own organizations. In this way they are able in most cases to get a rough idea of what will prove acceptable to the Budget Bureau, the President and his advisers, and the appropriations subcommittees in Congress.[8]

Thus, from March through July, the agencies and departments prepare for submission of their draft budget proposals to the Budget Bureau. Prior to the submission date, the agency or department usually has its own preview, when internal drafts of PM's, PFP's, and analytical studies are submitted, criticized, and revised.

Once the department or agency head is satisfied, the PM, PFP, and analytical studies are submitted to the Budget Bureau. There they are studied by the bureau staff; comments are made and revisions suggested. The agency then turns to preparation of its final set

[8] For further details of the motivations, aims, and policies of individual agencies, see Aaron Wildavsky, *The Politics of the Budgetary Process* (Little, Brown, 1964). Chap. 2.

of budget documents due on September 30. At this stage, the emphasis remains on *programs,* not dollar amounts.

The Fiscal Side of Budgeting

Although the budget process from February-September is mostly concerned with program analysis and issues, there is a continuing and parallel interest in the fiscal implications of the developing budget. Beginning with President Kennedy's term of office and continuing through the Johnson administration, the agencies concerned with the overall budget and its impact on the economy—the Budget Bureau, the Treasury, and the Council of Economic Advisers—have submitted periodic memorandums to the President, reviewing the economic situation and recent budget trends and revising the budget totals when necessary. This informal group, known as the "Troika," is regarded as having an important influence on budget and fiscal decision making. The President has periodic discussions with the Troika, sometimes joined by the chairman of the Federal Reserve Board (the group then becomes the "Quadriad"), and receives frequent memorandums from them. Out of these discussions and memorandums comes the President's decision on tax and expenditure policy.

During the summer months, the director of the bureau and his staff deal directly with the President and his advisers on emerging problems, initial clearance on major program decisions, and the overall revenue and expenditure outlook. By late summer the administration's overall budget policy for the forthcoming fiscal year begins to take shape.

Next comes a meeting of the director with each of the major agency heads to discuss the economic outlook, revenue, the total budget picture, the President's overall budget objective, and the agency's major budget items. After these meetings and further discussions with the President, in late summer, a "policy letter" is usually sent by the director of the Bureau of the Budget to agency and department heads giving information on various policy aims. More important, the general budget policy is translated into budget planning figures for some twenty agencies. These are not ceiling figures. Rather, the bureau is informing the agency that, in view of the administration's program, it is likely that the agency's budget will be somewhere near a certain figure. Agencies can bring in estimates exceeding the planning figure, but if they do, they must indicate where they could make cuts if required to get back down to the planning figure. It is at this point that the program and fiscal aspects of the budget process come together.

The Review Process

This is a crucial stage in the budget process. The agencies and departments conduct intensive examinations of their programs in light of the planning figures or budget directives that have been passed down to them and in light of the previous year's action by the appropriations committees of Congress. The agency or department that is well within its planning figure has no problems. (This is so rare as to be completely outside the experience of most career agency budget officers.) Most, however, face a difficult decision about where to cut (in the absence of specific directives), or whether to cut at all, or whether to fight it out by appealing to the Budget Bureau and, if necessary, the President himself.

Following the review within the department, estimates are submitted to the Bureau of the Budget, where they are reviewed by examiners and hearings are held, first with the agency official and then within the bureau, where the final decisions on recommendations to the President will be made. At these hearings, the department or agency presents and defends its programs and budget before the examiner and other staff members of the Budget Bureau.

Relations between agencies and the Budget Bureau are important at this stage, in particular the relation between each agency and the bureau's examiners assigned to it. On the one hand, the agency is reluctant to incur Budget Bureau disfavor, for the bureau's recommendations to the President do carry weight.[9] Congress usually exceeds the President's appropriations recommendations with some reluctance and more commonly cuts them. At the same time, the bureau cannot restrain the agencies too much, for "end runs" by agencies to Congress to get funds disapproved by the bureau are not unusual. So both parties are constrained, and the end result is usually somewhere between what each would prefer.

On the basis of the hearings and his knowledge of agency pro-

[9] It is important to note that the Budget Bureau is an "arm of the President"; it is not itself a formulator of policy except insofar as the director influences presidential decisions. It is a *staff* agency. However, under the law the director of the Bureau of the Budget is specifically given the power to review federal statistical programs. Interestingly enough, the bureau has about the same number of personnel today that it had in 1948.

grams, operations, and overall policies, the Budget Bureau examiner submits his recommendations to the director of the bureau, usually after informal consultation with the bureau staff. At this stage, the examiner's recommendations are subjected to a relatively formal evaluation by the Bureau of the Budget, which is called the "director's review." This is conducted by top staff members of the bureau —the director, the deputy director, and other officials, with the director usually serving as chairman.

Concurrent with the director's review is the last stage of executive budget preparation—presidential review of the budget as it emerges from the bureau and preparation of the annual budget document. After the President's review, his program decisions and approved "allowances" are sent to each agency head, who may then accept them or appeal them to the bureau, to the White House, or to the President himself. Another hearing on some of the issues is thus sometimes obtained. Also at this very hectic time, final conclusions are drawn concerning the economic outlook and prospective revenue, and these, together with the emerging expenditure estimates of the bureau, make it possible for the bureau, the Council of Economic Advisers, and the Treasury to recommend last-minute changes that will affect the size of the budget surplus or deficit. These changes may stimulate final appeals from the departments and agencies on decisions affecting their budgets.

During the third week in January—somewhat miraculously, considering the coordination and effort involved—the budget document and message are transmitted to Congress.

Congressional Authorization

The distinctive feature of the congressional phase of the budget process in the United States is the separation of expenditures and taxes and their consideration by different committees; there is almost no consideration of the administration's budget as a unified proposal. As a matter of fact, the legislative phase of budgeting is usually thought of only in terms of appropriations; taxation is viewed as a separate problem.

Terminology

Before we discuss the process by which the Congress affects the level of expenditures, the meaning of the terms "expenditure," "authorization," and "appropriation" must be clarified.

The budget document sets forth the President's proposals for the executive agencies regarding cash expenditures and new obligational authority during a fiscal year. The expenditures Congress finally approves reflect two separate stages of decision. First, it must approve the functions for which expenditures are to be made; this is called "authorization." That is, the Congress passes legislation authorizing specific activities, such as foreign aid and defense, but does not provide funds and sometimes does not even specify the amount of funds implied in the activity.[10] As a matter of custom, authorizing legislation must be enacted before funds are granted. Most federal programs now require *annual* authorization by Congress.

After a specific activity has been authorized, funds are provided in "appropriations"—legislation by Congress permitting a government agency or department to commit or obligate the government to certain expenditures, or what is commonly called "new obligational authority."[11] Since appropriations are not considered until authorizing legislation is passed, many agencies in recent years have received their appropriations late in the congressional session. When an agency does not receive its new appropriation before the old one lapses, it operates under a "continuing resolution" passed by Congress, which allows it to spend at the previous year's rate. Appropriations come in several forms, ranging from one-year appropriations, which allow an agency to incur obligations only during one fiscal year (the most common form) to no-year appropriations, which are available (for obligation and expenditure) until the purpose of the spending is accomplished. Generally, if the obligational authority is not used during the specified period, it lapses and is no longer available to the agency unless the Congress specifically reappropriates it.

Expenditures out of new obligational authority must be committed within a certain period but need not be actually paid within that period. Even in the case of one-year appropriations, the agency

[10] However, authorizing legislation does specify a maximum amount for 30 percent of total funds in the administrative budget.

[11] Obligational authority is also provided in two other forms: (1) authorizations to expend from debt receipts and (2) contract authorizations. However, these account for only a very small proportion of new obligational authority and will not be discussed separately here. See U.S. Bureau of the Budget, *The Budget of the United States Government, Fiscal Year 1962* (1961), p. 114, and *The Federal Budget as an Economic Document,* Prepared for the Joint Economic Committee, 87 Cong. 2 sess. (1962), pp. 8–13.

is given two more years to pay the bills (for example, after deliveries have been made).

Since new obligational authority may be granted for a period longer than the fiscal year, there is always a substantial carry-over of obligational authority from previous years. There is also a carry-over of unspent obligations from the previous year or two, that is, obligational authority that has been committed but under which no expenditures have actually been made. Thus the expenditure totals in a budget reflect expenditures expected to be made during the coming fiscal year out of uncommitted obligational authority—as well as unspent obligations—carried over from previous years and out of new obligational authority requested in the current budget, as is shown in Figure 3. Obligational authority and unspent obligations

FIGURE 3. Outlays for 1969 Related to Budget Authority

Total obligational authority available—$424.0 billion

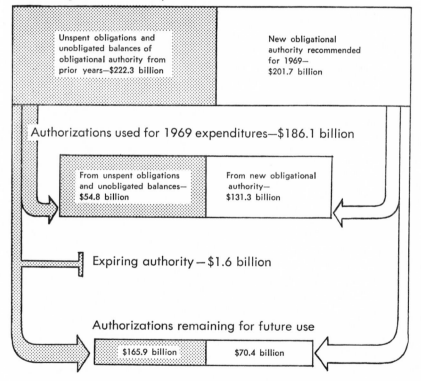

Source: *Budget for Fiscal 1969*, pp. 54–56.

carried over from previous years were $222.3 billion as of July 1, 1968. The 1969 budget requested $201.7 billion of new obligational authority, making a total of $424.0 billion available to the agencies. Of this, some $186.1 billion was expected to be spent during fiscal year 1969, $54.8 billion was available from unspent obligations and unobligated balances carried over and $131.3 billion from new obligational authority. With authorizations for $1.6 billion expiring, about $236.3 billion of obligational authority and unspent obligations would remain for years after fiscal 1969.

Appropriations legislation, then, determines new obligational authority for the coming year. Congress does not vote on expenditures by department or agency; it only determines new obligational authority. In fact, in the debate on appropriation bills, Congress does not consider the effect that congressional changes in the amounts of new obligational authority requested by the President will have on expenditures in the next fiscal year.

Congressional Consideration of Appropriations

Tax legislation may be initiated only by the House, and in practice, it has been customary for the House also to initiate appropriations legislation. The Senate has typically acted later and has assumed the role of a liberal counterweight to generally conservative appropriation action by the House.[12]

In the House the content of appropriations measures generally reflects the decisions of the House Committee on Appropriations and, more specifically, its various subcommittees. The Appropriations Committee has fifty members—thirty from the majority and twenty from the minority. Its work is done largely in thirteen subcommittees of from five to eleven members each. Each subcommittee is responsible for reporting out one or, occasionally, two appropriations bills, of which there are thirteen or fourteen in each congressional session.

Tremendous power and authority rest with the various subcommittees and their chairmen. Each subcommittee holds hearings on

[12] In 1962 a dispute broke into the open between the House and Senate over initiating appropriations legislation. The House felt that it alone could originate such legislation, but the Senate disagreed. Other issues, such as where Senate-House conference committees on appropriations should meet, were also involved. This dispute over powers of origination was not resolved, and the House has continued to originate such legislation.

requests from particular agencies for obligational authority. The hearings have been closed to the public for many years, but a record of what is said is kept and usually printed, except for those portions that relate to national security. Testimony is generally confined to agency and bureau heads and their budget officers.[13] After the hearings the subcommittee goes into executive session and decides on the recommendations it will make for appropriations and restrictions on activities. The recommendations are usually accompanied by reasons for the subcommittee's action and by comments on the agency's programs, efficiency, and personnel.[14]

The subcommittee's recommendations and report are then sent to the full committee for action. They are rarely discussed or even studied in detail; the full committee almost automatically approves the recommendations of the subcommittee and sends them on as a bill to the House, where they are debated with the House sitting as a committee of the whole. On the floor the chairman of the subcommittee acts as floor manager; extended debate is rare, and the bill usually passes expeditiously.[15]

Formerly, the Senate did not begin hearings on an appropriations bill until the House bill neared passage. Now, however, the Senate sometimes begins hearings on the same subject even before the House bill is written. As in the House, the initial work is done in the subcommittees (of which there are twelve) of the Appropriations Committee. Also as in the House, they hold hearings, mark up the bill, and send it to the full committee; and here, too, the recommendations of the subcommittees are almost always accepted by the full committee.

When holding hearings, the Senate subcommittees often used to resemble courts of appeal. Agencies and departments often relied on

[13] This is only because usually no one else asks to be heard. Subcommittees would schedule other witnesses advocating specific expenditure changes if they requested a hearing.

[14] The appropriations subcommittees have not reacted uniformly to PPBS. Further, the variation in their reaction has been reflected in no small degree in that of the agencies or departments that are dependent on them for appropriations. Where the subcommittee chairman is favorable to PPBS, agency use of it is encouraged and the subcommittee hearings will even be "program oriented." Attention will be focused on the program memorandum and analytic studies of the agency. Some subcommittee chairmen, however, have not fully accepted PPBS, and this has slowed their agencies' adoption of it and staffing for it.

[15] See Jesse Burkhead, *Government Budgeting* (John Wiley, 1956), pp. 98–99.

the Senate to restore cuts made by the House. But since the Senate began holding some of its hearings before the writing of the House bill in the same area, the aura of an appeals court is less prevalent. Still, after the House has passed, or at least written, its bill, senatorial questioning tends to center on differences between the amounts of obligational authority recommended in the President's budget (or those currently being requested by the agency witnesses) and the amounts granted by the House. More often than not, the Senate subcommittees restore portions of cuts made in the House.

On the floor of the Senate, discussion of appropriations measures is more extensive than in the House because of the privilege of unlimited debate. The Senate as a whole tends to be more generous in appropriations than the House; the final Senate version of appropriations bills is typically higher.

Senate-House differences on appropriations are reconciled by a conference committee, which seeks to reach a middle figure—one that the conferees can recommend to their parent bodies. The conference committee draft is returned to the House and Senate for further consideration. Usually it is accepted, but occasionally one or the other house rejects it and sends it back to conference.

After final congressional approval the measure is then sent to the President for his signature or veto. Particular agencies and departments are consulted if their appropriations raise the question of a veto, but appropriations bills are rarely vetoed. The bill must be accepted or rejected as a whole; item veto is not provided for by the Constitution. Although the President may not like the bill, he usually signs it, expressing disapproval of certain portions. A veto of the whole bill might endanger the acceptable portions the next time through Congress. Where appropriations are considered by the executive branch to be too low, it can request changes in the next budget after collecting additional supporting evidence and mobilizing the force of public opinion. Where unwanted funds are voted, the President can refuse to spend them, though this is rare and somewhat difficult to do. After all the appropriations measures are passed (which is generally very late in the year since Congress acts on appropriations last), the Budget Bureau prepares a press release which summarizes the final data on appropriations and expenditures resulting from congressional action and updates the revenue estimates of the original budget.

Execution of the Budget

How is the obligational authority granted by Congress to an agency or department converted into expenditures?

Apportionment and Allotment

When the appropriations bill is enacted, an appropriations warrant, drawn by the Treasury and countersigned by the General Accounting Office, is sent to the agency. The agency reviews and revises its budget in light of the appropriations bill and, within fifteen days of the appropriations bill's passage, submits to the Bureau of the Budget a request for apportionment. Apportionment basically means the rate at which the obligational authority can be used—the authority is usually apportioned by quarters over the period of the appropriation, both to insure that the obligational authority is not spent faster than Congress intended and to insure the most economical and effective use of the funds.

The Bureau of the Budget approves or revises the agency apportionment request; in effect, the bureau is the apportioning authority. The power of apportionment gives the executive some latitude in controlling the direction and timing of federal obligations, and it has on occasion been used to accelerate the rate of federal expenditure during a recession and to block programs the executive disapproves by refusing to use funds appropriated by Congress.[16]

Within the individual agencies, the use of the obligational authority apportioned by the bureau is controlled through a similar device. The breakdown of apportionment by organizational unit is called *allotment*.

Obligations Incurred and Expenditures

With minor exceptions, the various agencies actually incur obligations only after apportionment by the Bureau of the Budget.[17] Incurring obligations, however, does not necessarily mean immediate

[16] See "Federal Fiscal Behavior during the Recession of 1957–58," Bureau of the Budget Staff Report (multilithed; Jan. 13, 1967); statements of Walter Heller and David E. Bell in *January 1961 Economic Report of the President and the Economic Situation and Outlook,* Hearings before the Joint Economic Committee, 87 Cong. 1 sess. (1961); and *Economic Report of the President* (1962).

[17] See *The Federal Budget as an Economic Document,* p. 14.

cash expenditures. In some cases, the expenditure of funds virtually coincides with the incurring of obligations; in others, the actual expenditure of funds may lag considerably behind.

In two kinds of commitment, the time lag between obligations and expenditures is very short. Expenditures for the purchase of existing assets (except land, where the lag may be considerable), social security benefits, veterans' pensions, public assistance grants to states, unemployment compensation, some farm subsidies, and other subsidies involving no use of productive resources typically coincide with, or are very close to, the incurring of the obligations. Government expenditures for services (in particular, those of government employees) also typically occur close to the time of commitment.

But when the federal government contracts with the private sector to employ resources on its behalf—that is, when the federal government buys goods and services produced by the private sector— the lag of expenditures behind obligations may be substantial. This lag is both administrative and technological; it takes private producers time to draw plans, negotiate with subcontractors, and deliver the product.[18] Some of the economic impact on the private sector thus occurs long before actual delivery of goods and payment, since the producers must employ resources in order to produce goods.[19]

Expenditures

When they occur, expenditures are generally made from Treasury deposits at the twelve Federal Reserve Banks, which are part of the "Account of the Treasurer of the United States." This account consists mostly of the Treasury checking accounts at the twelve Federal Reserve Banks and at commercial banks. Federal disbursing officers make payment by issuing checks against the Federal Reserve Bank accounts on the basis of vouchers approved by certifying officers of the various agencies; the amount that can be issued is set

[18] See *The Federal Budget as an Economic Document*, pp. 18–21; and Murray Weidenbaum, "The Federal Government Spending Process," in Joint Economic Committee, *Federal Expenditure Policy for Economic Growth and Stability*, 85 Cong. 1 sess. (1957), p. A35. To the extent that there are progress payments or advance payments, the time lag is reduced. It should be noted that when the government buys goods offered for general sale to the public, which are generally quickly available from inventories, the lag is much less significant than when the government places an order for goods produced to its specifications.

[19] See Weidenbaum, "The Federal Government Spending Process," for a discussion of this point.

by the agency's obligational authority and the apportionment of it by the Bureau of the Budget. These checks are usually deposited in commercial banks, which then receive a credit to their Federal Reserve Bank accounts. The Federal Reserve Bank charges the Treasury account with the amount of the check and sends the check to the Treasury, where the checks that have been cashed are verified against the record of checks that have been issued.

It is the Treasury's responsibility to maintain adequate working balances at the Federal Reserve Banks to meet payments as they occur. For this purpose, amounts are funneled by the Treasury into Federal Reserve accounts from deposits at commercial banks made directly by district officers of the Internal Revenue Service and from receipts from debt issues.

Audit

The individual agencies and departments are responsible for insuring that the obligations they incur, and the resulting expenditures, are legal with respect to authorizing and appropriations legislation. The Congress, however, obtains an independent check through the General Accounting Office, which is headed by the comptroller general. The GAO audits the books of the administrative officers responsible for the custody and use of public funds. It has also played an important role in supervising the accounting systems of agencies and departments and in insuring that the methods of reporting result in full disclosure of the receipt and use of funds.

Three major types of audits are made by GAO. Recently, the *comprehensive audit* has become the most important. This audit concentrates on the accounting and reporting system used by a particular agency and checks transactions selectively. The *general audit* examines the accounts of agency disbursing and certifying officers to determine the legality of each transaction. If illegal or improper handling of receipts or expenditures is discovered, recovery procedures are instituted against the responsible officer. The *commercial audit* is applied to government corporations and enterprises. No recovery is possible in this case, but Congress is informed of questionable or improper practices.

The results of GAO audits are transmitted to Congress by the comptroller general. The results of special investigations of particular agencies and the annual report are referred to the House and Senate Committees on Government Operations.

Improvements in the Budget Process

As described in this chapter, budget procedures and the budget process reflect a number of improvements made in the last twenty years or so, most of them in the executive phase of the budget.

Changes in the Budget Document

First, the budget process has been improved considerably by changes in the budget document itself.

BUDGET MESSAGE IMPROVEMENT. A comparison of budget messages of recent years with that of 1947 shows that much greater emphasis is now being placed on the relation of federal finances to conditions in the national economy. Graphs have been introduced to explain this relationship. At the same time, the budget message has been considerably shortened.

A MORE COMPACT BUDGET VOLUME. The budget for the fiscal year 1963 (presented in January 1962) was a major improvement over previous budget documents, which were printed on outsize pages, about the thickness of a large-city telephone directory, and filled with thousands of detailed schedules. The 1963 budget, in about 300 pages of ordinary book size, included the facts and figures most users of the budget normally need, and relegated the details of appropriations proposals and programs used by the congressional committees to an appended volume. This procedure has been followed in subsequent budgets.

THE BUDGET IN BRIEF. Beginning in January 1950 the Bureau of the Budget has published each year a pamphlet presenting in popular form some of the most significant data relating to the budget and federal finance.

SPECIAL ANALYSES. The budget document has also been improved by the addition of several special analyses. Since 1942 the budget has included an analysis of the cash budget and its relationship to the administrative budget. The budget transmitted in January 1950, and succeeding budgets, contained an analysis of "investment, operating, and other expenditures," which divides budget expenditures into additions to federal assets, expenditures for nonfederal physical assets and other developmental purposes, current expenses for aids and special services, and other current operating expenses. The 1963 budget presented for the first time an analysis of federal receipts and expenditures on a national income accounts basis. Other special analyses have dealt with federal aid to state and local governments, federal credit programs, federal research and development programs, and federal government statistical programs.

OTHER CHANGES IN THE BUDGET DOCUMENT. Other changes have also markedly improved the budget. The budgets of all agencies were first broken down by program or activity in 1950, which made congressional appraisal easier, and in the same year a narrative statement of the results expected from each expenditure of funds was introduced. Recommendations for new obligational authority were first totaled as a separate category as recently as seventeen years ago. A comparison of unspent obligational authority, new obligational authority, and expenditures was included beginning with the January 1954 budget. Obligations incurred were given separate treatment in the January 1958 budget but were not summarized in a table by agency until the January 1962 budget. Also introduced in the 1962 budget was a recapitulation of employment for the government as a whole.

Improvements in the Executive Phase of Budgeting

PROGRAM BUDGETING. The recent effort to institute a program-planning-budgeting system was discussed at some length earlier in this chapter. It holds promise of being one of the most significant improvements in the executive phase of the budget process in recent decades.

The difficulties in program evaluation are many. The very nature of government—taking from some and giving to others—makes calculations of the costs and benefits of particular programs inevitably imprecise. The benefits, or output, of government programs are particularly difficult to measure in the absence of tools like market tests in the private sector. Nevertheless, analysis built on shaky assumptions and heroic simplifications provides a better basis for program choices than no analysis at all. Although benefits cannot be quantified, program objectives can be defined and the different means of achieving them can be analyzed, which at least allows government to spend its funds in the most efficient way, given its overall goals.

The most significant effects of PPBS in the short run are likely to be the pressure it brings to bear on agencies and departments to try to be analytical in making their spending recommendations, and the objective criteria for program decisions it gives agency and department heads. These alone represent a great step forward from years past, when intuitive judgment, the built-in impetus of programs, or simple political pressure was the base for such choices.

THE "TROIKA." As noted previously, beginning with President Kennedy's term of office and continuing in the Johnson administration, those agencies concerned with the overall budget and its impact on the economy—the Budget Bureau, the Treasury, and the Council of Economic Advisers—have submitted periodic memorandums to the President, reviewing the economic situation and recent budget trends and revising the budget totals when necessary. This Troika improves the budget process by keeping the chief executive continually informed about the economic situation and its implications for the budget, as well as the impact of the budget on the economy.

ORAL TESTIMONY ON THE OVERALL BUDGET. In addition to the improvements in the budget process, the presentation of the budget to Congress has also been improved in recent years through oral testimony by the director of the Budget Bureau and the secretary of the Treasury before one of the appropriations committees of Congress and the Joint Economic Committee. This procedure enables the committee to gain some understanding of the total budget picture before it acts on the specific pieces assigned to the various subcommittees.

Efforts To Improve the Congressional Phase of Budgeting

The procedures used by Congress in carrying out its responsibilities to appropriate federal funds—to control the purse strings—have not changed basically for many decades, certainly not in the last thirty or forty years. Two efforts have been made to effect fundamental changes. The Legislative Reorganization Act of 1946 provided for a Joint Committee on the Legislative Budget, which was to meet early in each session of Congress, consider the President's budget proposal in light of economic conditions and efficiency, and set an annual ceiling on appropriations. The committee died after it was unable to agree on a ceiling in 1947 and after its 1948 ceiling was not enforced.

A bill providing for the consolidation of all general appropriations into one omnibus appropriation act for action by the House, the Senate, and the President was introduced in 1950. The procedure was tried in that year, but the act did not pass the Senate until August 4 and was not signed into law until September 6. Both because the delay was attributed to the new omnibus procedure (although it is not clear just how the appropriations process was delayed) and because it did not give the President the power to reject parts of the bill without rejecting the whole, it was abandoned in 1951.

Weaknesses in the Budget Process

The changes in the budget process, particularly on the executive side, have been notable, as the discussion above suggests. However, there are still weaknesses in the overall budget process, which have been pointed out by various groups and individuals. Many of them concern the legislative role in budget making.

Coordination of Expenditure and Revenue Decisions by Congress

The budget is now taken up by Congress as a series of separate and unrelated parts. Taxes and expenditures are decided separately by separate committees in each house, and although the bills on taxes and appropriations must be passed in votes of the whole House and whole Senate, there is little evidence that the close relationships of the two groups of bills are considered by the legislators.

Some way should be found to insure that Congress considers the budget as a whole and the relation of expenditures to revenues. As was indicated above, the Legislative Reorganization Act of 1946 sought to accomplish this with the Joint Committee on the Legislative Budget, which was to recommend a firm limit on total expenditures in a concurrent resolution after due consideration of revenues and the economic outlook and before the various appropriations subcommittees began work on individual appropriations measures. For various reasons, the joint committee did not work out satisfactorily: it was too large, and an overall expenditures limit was difficult to implement.

The Committee for Economic Development has recommended a joint budget policy conference.[20] This group, to include members of the congressional leadership, majority and minority representatives from the revenue and appropriations committees of both houses, and the Joint Economic Committee, would study the budget as a whole and issue a report, with the aim of providing communication among the revenue and appropriations committees of the two houses and the Joint Economic Committee.

Whatever is the best organizational solution, this weakness in the present budget process seems obvious to many, and some corrective action needs to be taken.

Coordination of Appropriations Decisions

Under present procedures, appropriations are determined in both the House and the Senate in some thirteen separate appropriations bills, with little consideration by the subcommittee responsible for each bill of the effect on total new obligational authority, total obligations to be incurred, or the likely level of total expenditures. The benefits and costs of the programs involved in each of the thirteen bills are not considered in relation to the benefits and costs of programs involved in the other bills. Thus the individual congressman is not encouraged to do what he should do—look at appropriations and expenditures as a whole and compare alternative programs in order to decide, on the basis of their costs and benefits, what changes should be made. This unsatisfactory situation results in part from the fact that the appropriations subcommittees dominate appropriations decisions in both houses of Congress; seldom does either full committee make a decision as a unit.

The problem might be solved if meetings were held of the chairmen of the various appropriations subcommittees and if the two houses considered appropriations bills at more nearly the same time, as the Committee for Economic Development suggested.[21] The appropriations committees of Congress might also be encouraged to consider total appropriations if the President were given an *item*

---

[20] Committee for Economic Development, *Control of Federal Government Expenditures* (CED, 1955), pp. 15–16.

[21] *Ibid..* pp. 17–18.

veto—the power to veto parts of appropriations bills that have passed both houses of Congress without vetoing the whole bill, as the CED also suggested.[22] Whatever particular institutional changes are made, some means must be found to enable Congress to look at the total appropriation as well as the parts.

Flexibility in Changing Expenditures and Taxes

A number of groups and individuals have argued that the President should be given more power to change, at least temporarily, total federal spending and/or tax rates. The argument usually stems from a desire for a procedure that would be immediately effective in evening out the ups and downs of the economy and attacking the accompanying problems of unemployment and inflation. Under present arrangements, it usually takes a very long time for Congress to approve a change in tax rates or spending authority.[23] Thus timely action to halt a recession or check an inflation may be precluded by the long time lag between a decision to do something and getting Congress to do it.

In their economic reports from January 1962 through January 1965 President Kennedy and President Johnson proposed that the President be given some form of standby authority to make temporary reductions in individual income tax rates and to accelerate expenditures. Congress has never acted on these proposals and they were not proposed in the 1966 and 1967 economic reports.

Several other proposals to allow the executive more flexibility in influencing tax rates and spending have been put forth in the last two or three decades. They have met with little success. The Congress is very reluctant to delegate its control over taxes and spending, even for temporary changes, to the President. Although many observers agree that such standby authority would make possible effective use of the budget as an economic tool, the outlook is not bright.

[22] *Ibid.,* p. 18.

[23] The 1963 tax cut took approximately one year and three months after its proposal by President Kennedy to clear Congress and become law. It took 18 months for the 1968 tax surcharge to be enacted.

CHAPTER IV

The Record: Federal Spending and Taxes

A DISCUSSION OF federal budget policy can benefit from the perspective provided by a brief look at the record of federal spending and taxation over the last 178 years, in particular in the period since 1930. Our review will include the record of budget deficits and surpluses in this period and an analysis of the extent to which, and reasons why, actual expenditures and receipts have differed from budget estimates.

Trends in Federal Expenditures

Although Americans are somewhat inured to the colossal and the spectacular, the growth of federal government expenditures over the last century and three-quarters is still impressive. In 1794, for example, the federal government spent about $7 million on a cash budget basis. In fiscal 1967 federal expenditures on a cash basis were over $155 billion, or more than 22,000 times those of 1794.

The pattern of this striking growth in federal expenditures is shown in Figure 4.[1] The most obvious influence on the pattern has

[1] Cash budget expenditure figures are used because they are the only ones available for the period discussed here.

been war. Large expansions of federal spending occurred during the War of 1812, the Civil War, World War I, and World War II. The trend of federal expenditures over the past 178 years may be described as a series of plateaus. Wars have pushed federal spending sharply upward. With the return of peace, expenditures have fallen but never to prewar levels because the wars left a heritage of interest and veterans' expenses. Between wars, expenditures have shown long periods of relative stability or even decline. But when another war has come along, they have been forced up, eventually leveling off at a higher plateau.

The growth of federal expenditures can best be placed in perspective by comparison with growth in other economic magnitudes over time. Over the 178-year period, the general price level has approximately tripled, or to put it another way, the value of the dollar today is perhaps one-third its value in 1790. If we allow for changes in the general price level by expressing government expenditures in

FIGURE 4. Federal Cash Expenditures, 1794–1967[a]

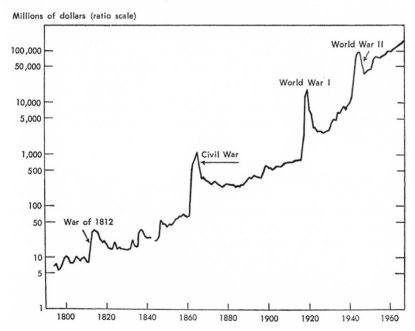

Sources: Data for 1794–1947 are from M. Slade Kendrick, *A Century and a Half of Federal Expenditures*, Occasional Paper 48 (National Bureau of Economic Research, 1955), Table B-1 (pp. 74–77); data for 1948–67 are from U.S. Bureau of the Budget, *Budget of the United States Government* for fiscal years 1961, 1963, 1965, 1966, and 1969. The 1843 data cover the period January–June 1843 only.
[a] Calendar years through 1842; fiscal years thereafter.

FIGURE 5. Total and Per Capita Federal Cash Expenditures in 1926 Prices, 1794–1967[a]

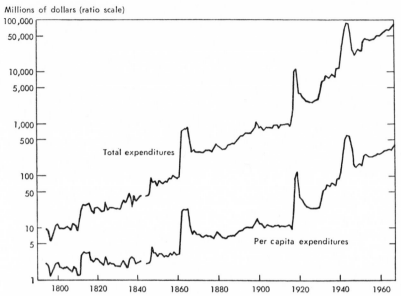

Sources: Expenditures in 1926 prices for 1794–1952 are from Kendrick, *A Century and a Half of Federal Expenditures*, pp. 79–82. For 1953–64 they were computed from data used for Figure 4 and wholesale price index data taken from various issues of the *Federal Reserve Bulletin* and the *Economic Report of the President*. Per capita expenditures in 1926 prices for 1794–1952 are from Kendrick, *A Century and a Half of Federal Expenditures*, pp. 84–87. For 1953–67 they were computed by dividing expenditures in 1926 prices by populations taken from various issues of *Statistical Abstract of the United States*.

[a] Calendar years through 1842; fiscal years thereafter.

1926 prices, the rise in spending is much less formidable, as Figure 5 shows. Whereas expenditures expressed in current prices grew 22,000 times their level in 1790, expenditures expressed in 1926 prices expanded about 8,400 times. Expenditures expressed on a per capita basis are another useful measure. If we make allowance for a fifty-fold growth in population since 1790, the growth in expenditures in 1926 prices for each person has been 170 times the earlier level.

Perhaps the most significant measure of the growth of federal spending is the ratio of total federal spending to national output, or gross national product (GNP). Many types of federal spending can be expected to increase as the nation's economy expands—more highways have to be built to transport more output, growing urban areas require more post offices, and so on. Of course, there are other influences on spending, for example, that of the international situation on defense spending.

In any case, comparing federal expenditures with GNP is one way of measuring the importance of the government in the total economy. Of total federal spending, only the component "government purchases of goods and services" indicates the actual amount of resources absorbed by the government. The other components—transfer payments, net interest, subsidies, and grants to states and localities—represent income channeled through the federal government to the private sector or to the states and their subdivisions to spend. However, the sum of these expenditures can usefully be compared with GNP, since they are all part of total federal activity in the economy.

Figure 6 shows a rise in federal expenditures relative to GNP over the period 1869–1967. From 5 percent in 1869, and a low of 2 percent in 1912–13, the percentage has risen to around 20 in recent years. As the figure makes clear, most of the rise has taken place since 1930. Except for the World War I years, federal expenditures remained about the same relative to GNP from 1869 to 1930. There was a rise during the 1930's and a very sharp rise during World War II. The percentage fell back somewhat after World War II but has remained near 20 ever since. Purchases of goods and services, an important component of government expenditures, have increased at a slower pace because of the growth in importance of the federal trust funds.

Some light can be shed on the causes of the rise in this percentage since 1930 by classifying federal expenditures into "war-connected" and "other" and seeing how these two classes have behaved relative to GNP. War-connected expenditures can be defined as military expenditures (including military grants to other countries), veterans' expenditures, and interest on the federal debt. The last is included because the bulk of presently outstanding debt was issued to finance war. Figure 7 presents the relationship between war-connected and other expenditures and GNP since 1929. The figure shows that, although the rise in federal expenditures is in considerable measure a reflection of the rise in war-connected expenditures, there was also a noticeable rise in other expenditures in relation to GNP, from less than 1 percent in 1929 to over 9 percent in 1967.

War-connected expenditures rose sharply relative to GNP during World War II and then fell back drastically after the war as the country engaged in rapid demobilization. They rose again in 1950

FIGURE 6. Federal Cash Expenditures as a Percentage of Gross National Product, 1869–1967[a]

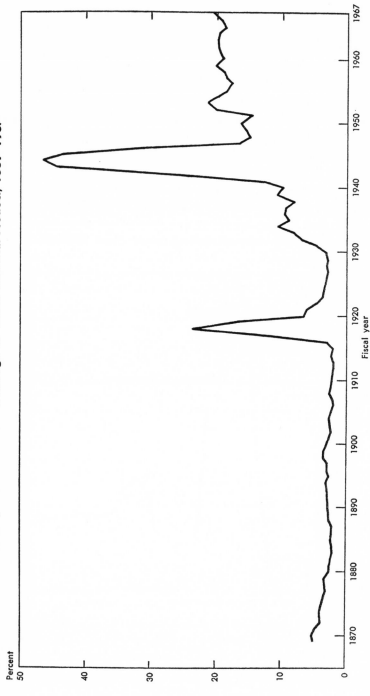

Percent

Fiscal year

Sources: Data for 1869–1947 are from Kendrick, *A Century and a Half of Federal Expenditures*, pp. 10–11, and data for 1948–67 are from the U.S. Bureau of the Budget

a. Data are for fiscal years.

with the advent of the Korean War and later with the cold war, remaining at about 11–12 percent of GNP through the early 1960's. Since 1965, however, war-connected expenditures have been smaller relative to GNP, even with the sharp increases in military outlays connected with the Vietnam conflict. (As Figure 7 shows, war-connected expenditures are sharply down relative to GNP in fiscal years 1966 and 1967 if the costs of Vietnam are excluded.) These outlays rose from $103 million in 1965 to $20 billion in 1967.

Other kinds of federal expenditures rose sharply relative to GNP during the 1930's, first under the impact of various relief and recov-

FIGURE 7. Federal War-Connected and Other Cash Expenditures as a Percentage of Gross National Product, Fiscal Years 1929–67

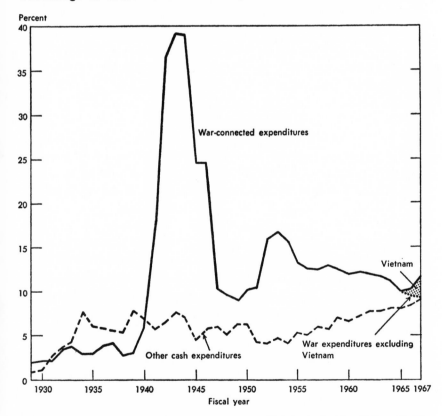

Sources: Kendrick, *A Century and a Half of Federal Expenditures,* p. 77; *Budget for Fiscal Year 1969,* pp. 83, 540, 543; and previous budgets. Data for 1958–67 are based on the new unified budget concept.

ery programs designed to combat the very deep depression into which the country had plunged and later when welfare programs such as old age and survivors' insurance and unemployment compensation were instituted. During World War II, however, and for most of the first ten years afterward, the percentage remained almost level. In 1954, these kinds of expenditures again began to rise faster than GNP, and in 1967 they reached the all-time high of 9 percent of GNP.

Thus, the striking change since 1930 has been the increase in both war-connected and other expenditures relative to GNP. The explanation for the increase in war-connected expenditures is obvious, but that for other kinds of outlays may be less so.

What has caused the increase in other expenditures relative to GNP during the last thirty years? Initially it reflected a host of depression-induced relief and welfare measures, as was mentioned above.[2] However, the relief and public works measures came to an end as the country recovered from the depression and began to prepare for World War II in the late 1930's and early 1940's. And expenditures for agriculture and unemployment benefits also fell as the economy moved toward full employment during World War II.

Since World War II, and more particularly since 1954, these kinds of expenditures have risen in large part because of the expansion of programs begun in the 1930's but also because of changed economic conditions which would have raised expenditures in any case. Figure 8 shows the distribution of other kinds of expenditures for the fiscal years 1948–67, by dollar amounts and in percentages. It shows that the sharpest dollar increase in expenditures over the postwar period has been in the health, labor, and welfare category. Cash expenditures on these functions rose from $3 billion in 1948 to $40 billion in 1967. This was mainly the result of increases in old age and survivors' insurance payments and unemployment compensation benefits, which accounted for about 80 percent of the in-

[2] M. Slade Kendrick (*A Century and a Half of Federal Expenditures*, Occasional Paper 48 [National Bureau of Economic Research, 1955], pp. 32–33) estimates that 36 percent of total federal expenditures for the period 1930–41 were for programs begun after 1930 in response to the depression (relief, public works, aid to agriculture, social security, and unemployment benefits), and in 1935 this proportion was as high as 57 percent.

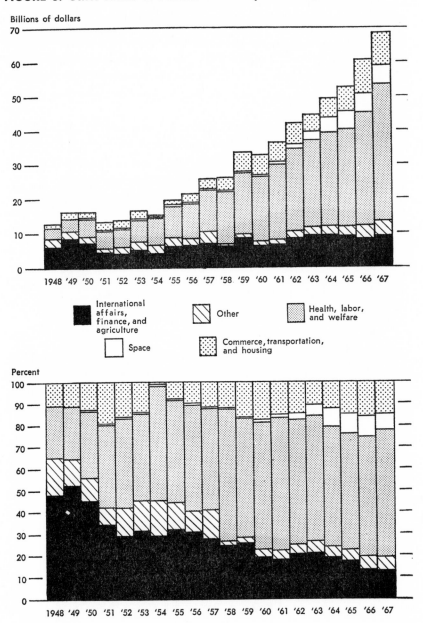

FIGURE 8. Other Kinds of Federal Cash Expenditures, 1948–67

Billions of dollars

Legend:
- International affairs, finance, and agriculture
- Space
- Other
- Commerce, transportation, and housing
- Health, labor, and welfare

Percent

Source: *Budget for Fiscal Year 1969*, p. 540. Data for 1958–67 are based on the new unified budget concept.

Table 8. Federal Receipts from the Public for Selected Years, 1792–1967[a]

Year	Individual income taxes	Corporation income taxes	Excise taxes	Employment taxes	Estate and gift taxes	Customs	Unemployment insurance deposits	Premiums for insurance and retirement	Other	Total
In millions of dollars										
1792	—	—	—	—	—	3.4	—	—	0.2	3.7
1830	—	—	—	—	—	21.9	—	—	2.9	24.8
1860	—	—	—	—	—	53.2	—	—	2.9	56.1
1910	—	21.0	269.0	—	—	333.7	—	—	51.9	675.5
1930	1,146.8	1,263.4	565.1	—	64.8	587.0	—	—	550.8	4,177.9
1967	61,526.0	33,971.0	13,719.0	n.a.	2,978.0	1,901.0	n.a.	n.a.	n.a.	153,596.0
As a percentage of total										
1792	—	—	—	—	—	94	—	—	6	100
1830	—	—	—	—	—	88	—	—	12	100
1860	—	—	—	—	—	95	—	—	5	100
1910	—	3	40	—	—	49	—	—	8	100
1930	27	30	14	—	2	14	—	—	13	100
1967	40	22	9	n.a.	2	1	n.a.	n.a.	n.a.	100

Sources: Data for 1792–1930 are from U.S. Bureau of the Census, Historical Statistics of the United States, Colonial Times to 1957 (1960), and Annual Report of the Secretary of the Treasury on the State of the Finances, various issues; data for later years are from the U.S. Bureau of the Budget.
n.a. Not available.
[a] Data for 1792 and 1830 are for the calendar year. All other figures are for fiscal years. Figures may not add to totals because of rounding.

crease in this category. Other significant increases have occurred in expenditures for commerce and housing and for agriculture.

In summary, the striking feature in the record of federal expenditures is their rise relative to GNP since 1930, partly because of wars, including the cold war, but also because of an apparent tendency for expenditures for other kinds of governmental activities to remain high.

Trends in Federal Receipts

Three trends stand out when federal receipts over the last 178 years are studied. First, there has been a massive growth in receipts paralleling the growth in expenditures. Second, customs receipts (taxes on imported goods), which were of overwhelming importance as a source of revenue until the Civil War, have since dwindled to very minor significance. That is, there has been a marked shift from external to internal revenue. Third, individual and corporate income taxes and employment taxes have become dominant as sources of revenue.

These trends are portrayed in Table 8. Although total receipts did not parallel expenditures exactly—the government ran surpluses in some years and deficits in others—the general order of increase was the same. Customs duties provided about 90 percent of federal receipts in 1792, 1830, and 1860 but less and less thereafter, until in 1967 they accounted for about 1 percent. The table shows the remarkable rise of individual and corporate income tax receipts, from nothing before 1910, when there were no such taxes (except during the Civil War), to 62 percent in 1967.

Employment taxes, those imposed on payrolls to finance social security, have also risen in importance. They accounted for about 19 percent of federal revenue in 1967 (precise data on which to base this percentage are not available after 1966). Another relatively new feature of the federal tax system, estate and gift taxes, has made a minor contribution to the increase in revenue. Finally, although the relative importance of receipts from federal excise taxes has not increased since 1930, their absolute growth has been significant; many of these taxes were introduced during World War II and remained in effect until 1965.

Thus the federal revenue system has undergone substantial change as the expenditures of the federal government have in-

FIGURE 9. Federal Cash Deficits and Surpluses, 1792–1967

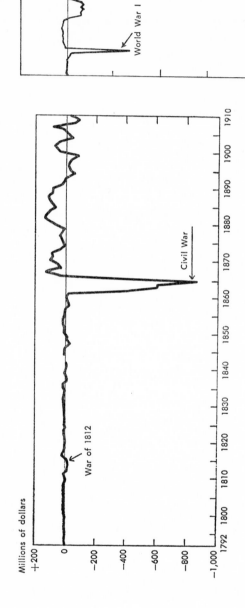

Sources: Expenditure data for 1792–1964 are from the sources given for Figure 4 (p. 49). Receipts data for 1792–1929 are from U.S. Bureau of the Census, *Historical Statistics of the United States,* Series Y254; and for 1930–67, from the U.S. Bureau of the Budget.

creased. Since World War I the tax system has been revolutionized through the adoption and increased importance of income taxation. Reliance on income taxes has improved the productivity of the national revenue system, and in general it has been judged a fair method of raising revenue. While there are a number of difficult problems involved in federal taxation, the tax structure of the United States, as compared with those of most other countries, ranks high in fairness as well as in productivity and compliance.

Cash Deficits and Surpluses

Since 1792 the federal government has run cash deficits in 75 years and surpluses in 101 years. The pattern of deficits and surpluses over this 176-year period is shown in Figure 9. As is clear from the figure, the large deficits have, for the most part, been incurred in periods of war, although there have been a number of nonwar deficits, notably those of the 1930's.

Figure 9 also shows that deficits are not peculiar to the period since the 1930's, as is sometimes suggested. In the period 1792–1920, there were 46 deficit years and 82 surplus years, or a deficit in roughly one out of three years. The ratio is much higher, of course, for the more recent period: since 1930 there have been 9 years of surplus and 29 years of deficits. Since World War II, there have been 8 surplus years out of 20.

Since 1792 the deficits have been cumulatively greater than the surpluses, and thus the federal government has accumulated a sizable public debt. In December 1966 the total federal debt was $329.8 billion.

Comparison of Estimated and Actual Receipts and Expenditures

Observers in the news media and politicians often comment on the disparity between budget estimates of expenditures or receipts (or deficits or surpluses) and the actual results. The implication is that budget estimates are not to be trusted or that they are even twisted for political purposes.

A look at the record might incline one to agree that budget estimates are unreliable. Table 9 shows estimated and actual receipts

Table 9. Comparison of Federal Budget Estimates with Actual Receipts and Expenditures, 1947–67

(In billions of dollars)

Fiscal year	Receipts				Expenditures			
	Estimate	Actual	Difference	Difference as percentage of actual receipts	Estimate	Actual	Difference	Difference as percentage of actual expenditures
	(1)	(2)	(3)	(4)	(5)	(6)	(7)	(8)
1947	29,462	39,786	10,324	25.9	33,074	39,032	5,958	15.3
1948	36,894	41,375	4,481	10.8	36,692	32,955	— 3,737	—11.3
1949	43,894	37,663	— 6,231	—16.5	39,086	39,474	388	1.0
1950	40,362	36,422	— 3,940	—10.8	41,235	39,544	— 1,691	— 4.3
1951	36,643	47,480	10,837	22.8	41,776	43,970	2,194	5.0
1952	54,299	61,287	6,988	11.4	71,156	65,303	— 5,853	— 9.0
1953	69,987	64,671	— 5,316	— 8.2	84,373	74,120	—10,253	—13.8
1954	67,827	64,420	— 3,407	— 5.3	77,749	67,537	—10,212	—15.1
1955	62,461	60,209	— 2,252	— 3.7	65,389	64,389	— 1,000	— 1.6
1956	59,685	67,850	8,165	12.0	62,093	66,224	4,131	6.2
1957	65,833	70,562	4,729	6.7	65,398	68,966	3,568	5.2
1958	73,053	68,550	— 4,503	— 6.6	71,240	71,369	129	0.2
1959	74,045	67,915	— 6,130	— 9.0	73,287	80,342	7,055	8.8
1960	77,100	77,763	663	0.9	77,030	76,539	— 491	— 0.6
1961	83,346	77,659	— 5,687	— 7.3	79,162	81,515	2,353	2.9
1962	81,666	81,409	— 257	— 0.3	80,232	87,787	7,555	8.6
1963	85,500	86,376	876	1.0	94,311	92,642	— 1,669	— 1.8
1964	88,400	89,459	1,059	1.2	98,405	97,684	— 721	— 0.7
1965	93,000	93,072	72	a	97,900	96,507	— 1,393	— 1.4
1966	100,000	104,727	4,727	4.5	106,428	106,978	550	0.5
1967	116,995	115,849	— 1,146	— 1.0	126,729	125,718	— 1,011	— 0.8
Average of percentage differences				7.9				5.4

Source: U.S. Bureau of the Budget. The following items were deducted from original budget receipts and expenditure estimates and actual figures: (1) Railroad Retirement Account, 1947–54; (2) refunds of receipts and capital transfers, 1947; and (3) interfund transactions, 1948–67.

ᵃ Less than 0.5.

and expenditures and the differences between them. For the period 1947–67 the average annual error in estimating expenditures was some 5 percent of actual expenditures, and the average annual error in estimating receipts was almost 8 percent of actual receipts.[3] It should be remembered, however, that making estimates of receipts and expenditures involves forecasting international events and economic conditions for an eighteen-month period; the budget submitted in January is for the twelve-month period beginning the following July. In the six months from January to July, or at any time during the fiscal year, international upheavals or unexpected changes

[3] At the same time it is interesting to note that if we take algebraic averages of the errors in estimating receipts and expenditures over the period—where underestimates are canceled in part by overestimates—the average excess of actual receipts over estimated receipts is about 1.4 percent of actual receipts, and the average shortfall of actual expenditures below estimated expenditures is 0.3 percent of actual expenditures.

in economic conditions at home can drastically alter expenditure needs or the basis on which receipts are estimated. Further, when there is a change of administrations, the incoming President often requests Congress to change substantially the budget estimates submitted by the outgoing President.[4] And finally, unless the President is persuasive and powerful enough, the Congress may alter his budget program, with resulting substantial differences between requested and actual receipts and expenditures.

[4] President Eisenhower reduced expenditure requests for fiscal 1954 some $7 billion below estimates in the Truman budget for that year. The large gap between actual expenditures in fiscal 1954 and budget estimates is the result of the Eisenhower revision. For fiscal 1962 Eisenhower submitted a budget calling for $80.9 billion in expenditures. The incoming Kennedy administration decided a larger amount was needed, and a large supplemental request was submitted in the summer of 1961 to support the defense buildup at the time of the Berlin crisis. As a result, actual expenditures in fiscal 1962 exceeded the Eisenhower request by some $7 billion.

CHAPTER V

Federal Budget Policy
and the Economy

SINCE THE 1930's, it has been widely accepted that the federal budget can and should be used to level the ups and downs of the economy, that is, that federal budget policy should be an important part of economic stabilization policy. In the 1950's, in addition to its stabilizing influence, federal budget policy was judged to be a stimulant to economic growth. Still later, in the early 1960's, it was recognized that budget policy should also be concerned with the nation's balance of payments. These ideas have been refined and expanded, and now it might be said that the most important criterion for judging federal spending and taxing plans is their combined impact on employment, prices, economic growth, and the balance of payments. It is inevitable and right that those concerned with the federal budget, both in the executive branch and in Congress, should be concerned with its impact on the economy.

This chapter discusses the impact of budget policy on the nation's economy and how this impact must be taken into consideration when deciding on specific expenditure and tax policies.

The federal budget makes its impact on the nation's economy

62

largely through its effect on aggregate spending. Spending by consumers, businesses, and government (federal, state, and local) determines output, employment, prices, and the balance of payments. The federal government, through its taxing and spending policies, can effect changes in aggregate spending and therefore in output, employment, prices, and the balance of payments. In fact, the government's policies affect the economy whether the government plans it or not, and so an understanding of the effect is important when budget and taxing plans are formulated.

Planned Spending

The effect of spending on output, employment, and prices will be considered first; for the moment any balance-of-payments effects will be ignored. The nation's output, or gross national product (GNP), is the sum of spending by consumers, businesses, and government on goods and services produced domestically (that is, excluding imports), plus foreigners' purchases of goods produced in this country.[1] Consumers consume goods and services, business spends on capital goods and inventories (investment), and government purchases goods from private industry and the services of its employees. For any period, total spending, including business spending on inventories, always equals output. That is, to be included in the total, goods must by definition have been sold to government, consumers, businesses, and foreign countries or else have gone into business inventories. But what makes the output level for any period what it is? What causes it to change?

Suppose at some selected output level the planned or desired spending of consumers, businesses, government, and foreigners are added up, including planned additions to, or decreases in, invento-

[1] More precisely, gross national product is the total value of all currently produced final goods and services in the economy for some particular period whether they are sold at home or abroad. By "final" goods or services we mean goods or services that do not enter into the production of other goods; the production of "intermediate" goods—that is, goods used in the production of other goods or services—is excluded from this measure of the final product of the nation. An estimate is made of how much of each final good or service is produced in a given period; this amount is multiplied by the market price of that good to get the value. The two values—of goods sold at home and goods sold abroad—are then added to get the total value of current goods and services produced.

ries. Suppose also that what these sectors want to buy or add to inventories just equals the assumed output level. Under these circumstances, employment and output will continue at the desired level. What happens if consumers, government, businesses, or foreigners decide to spend more than before? Then total spending (including inventory accumulation) will be greater than output. Businesses will experience an unplanned reduction in their inventories, and to rebuild them they will seek to increase production, at least where this is possible. A decline in planned spending will produce the opposite effect: an unplanned increase in business inventories, leading to a reduction in output. *The crucial force determining level of output, then, is planned spending by consumers, businesses, government, and foreigners.*

Planned spending is therefore also the crucial force determining the level of employment and hence of unemployment, since employment of labor services tends to vary in the same direction as GNP.[2] More output requires more hours of labor, and lower output, fewer hours.

The relation of planned spending to prices and growth involves yet another concept: "potential" or "full employment" GNP. At any given time there is a maximum potential GNP that is consistent with full employment of the nation's labor supply. That is, given the size of the labor force, the average work-week and work-year, and the average productivity of labor per man-hour, there is a certain GNP that could be produced if the labor force were all employed, allow-

---

[2] Not all unemployment should cause concern. There is always an irreducible minimum of frictional unemployment, reflecting the fact that the economy does not work perfectly. "Normal" unemployment results from job switching, from the fact that vacant jobs and available workers are not always in the same place at the same time, and so on. The term "unemployment" will, therefore, be used here to mean unemployment in excess of normal, frictional unemployment. For more detail on the definition and measurement of frictional unemployment, see "The Extent and Nature of Frictional Unemployment," in *Study of Employment, Growth, and Price Levels,* Study Paper No. 6, Prepared for the Joint Economic Committee, 86 Cong. 1 sess. (November 1959).

How much unemployment can be considered to be merely frictional? There are differences of opinion on this question. Some say that no more than 2 percent unemployed can be considered frictional, but others are willing to accept higher figures. The majority opinion currently seems to hold that an unemployment rate of 2–3 percent of the labor force would represent frictional unemployment only. A rate of more than 3 percent, then, would clearly be a cause for concern.

ing for the usual frictional unemployment.[3] Full employment GNP obviously does not remain unchanged with the passage of time. The labor force will grow if the number of workers entering it is great enough to more than offset reductions in the work-week and work-year. Likewise, research and development and the addition of new capital equipment will raise labor productivity.

Actual GNP, which we have just seen is determined basically by the planned spending of consumers, businesses, and government, may equal full employment GNP or be lower or higher. If planned spending is greater than output at full employment, that is, if consumers, businesses, and government are trying to buy more output (at current prices) than can be produced, there will be what is called an "inflationary gap" between planned spending and full employment GNP, and prices will tend to rise. This effect is sometimes termed an "excess demand" inflation, indicating that at full employment or capacity output the money demand for goods and services is in excess of that required to purchase this output at current prices. Theories concerning inflation are very complex, and the speed and duration of inflation will not be analyzed in detail here. The essential fact to note is that when planned spending exceeds full employment GNP, prices tend to rise.

If, instead, planned spending is weak and actual GNP is clearly less than full employment GNP, unemployment can be expected, since employment varies with output and output is less than that required for full employment of the labor force. In this case there will be what is called a "deflationary gap."

The government can attack rising prices or unemployment by causing planned spending to vary. If the economy is bumping against full employment GNP and prices are rising, government may seek to restrain planned spending. If the economy is below full employment GNP, the government may seek to bolster spending. A policy affecting only planned spending, however, may not be sufficient to achieve stable prices and eliminate unemployment (above

[3] Full employment GNP is devised by multiplying the available labor supply by average labor productivity. The available labor supply is the total labor supply, less frictional unemployment, in man-hours. Suppose, for example, that the available labor supply is 160 billion man-hours (80 million workers working 40 hours a week 50 weeks a year). Then, if average productivity per man-hour were $5, full employment GNP would be $800 billion.

frictional unemployment) at the same time. As the economy moves close to full employment, there is an upward pressure on prices. Plants are pushed to capacity, overtime and third-shift work becomes necessary, inexperienced workers must be hired, and unit costs thus tend to rise. In addition, unions are likely to press for higher wages, and sellers having monopoly power may be more inclined to raise prices than to stabilize them.

Unless devices are available to restrain directly the upward pressure on prices and wages as the economy approaches full employment—in addition to the indirect means of affecting total planned spending—society may have to choose between some inflation and full employment or no inflation and less than full employment. All feasible combinations of the rate of unemployment and the rate of price increase are shown on the possibility curve in Figure 10. At point *A* the rate of price increase is zero, but the unemployment rate

FIGURE 10. A Possibility Curve of the Relationships between Unemployment and Prices

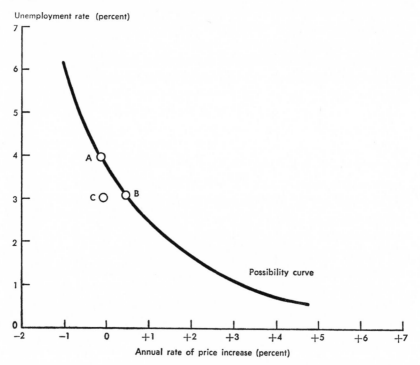

is 4 percent, which is a higher rate than can be accounted for by frictional unemployment. When the unemployment rate is 3 percent, as at *B,* there is no unemployment in excess of that usually considered frictional, but prices rise by some 0.5 percent per year. Society can choose any point on the possibility curve by altering total planned spending. However, points like *C,* where unemployment is 3 percent and the rate of inflation is zero, can be attained only if some type of wage-price policy is adopted which will restrain the upward tendency of prices and wages as total spending rises and pushes GNP toward the full employment level.

The shape and position of the possibility curve at any one time are thus determined by the structure of the economy and government wage-price policy. The curve may be changed through alterations in the basic characteristics of the economy, for example, by a weakening of union powers or a decrease in business monopoly power, or it may be changed by stronger or weaker policies on the part of government to affect prices and wages. But at any point in time, policy makers have to choose. In the above example, those who are most worried about inflation might choose point *A.* Those whose major worry is unemployment might choose *B.* Opinions will differ as to which is desirable, and no one answer is "right" in any absolute sense.

To simplify our analysis, we will assume throughout that there is no "tradeoff problem"—that the possibility curve passes through point *C* in Figure 10 and thus that the ideal domestic policy goals of full employment without inflation can be achieved by making actual GNP equal to full employment GNP. However, even if actual GNP and full employment GNP are equal during a certain period, without inflation, there is still the problem of growth. Suppose that during a particular year the economy is at a point where actual GNP equals full employment GNP. As the labor force and labor productivity increase, full employment GNP increases. In the next year, then, full employment GNP might be $50 billion greater. If private spending rises strongly, or if government budget policy is expansionary and total spending (at current prices) rises by more than $50 billion, inflation will result. On the other hand, if nothing occurs to increase private spending by $50 billion, or if the government takes no action, there will be a gap between planned spending and full employment GNP and a tendency for unemployment to develop. In short, just achieving full employment GNP at stable prices in a particular year is not enough; the economy is faced with the inexorable growth of full employment GNP, or potential output, which, if not matched closely by increases in spending by government, businesses, and consumers, can lead to either inflation or idle plant and equipment in industry and unemployment among the labor force.

The problem for policy makers so far as *domestic* objectives are concerned, then, is to see that planned spending by consumers, businesses, and government is such that the desired combination of employment and price level stability (among those combinations that are feasible) is achieved. This means that planned spending should be close to full employment GNP; if it is more, prices will rise, and if it is less, there will be unemployment. And the problem is continuous—the steady growth of full employment GNP calls for continuous action to assure the growth of planned spending.

Full employment GNP is to some extent within the scope of public policy. Although public policy cannot do much about the rate of growth of the labor force, at least in the short run, it can alter the average work-week and work-year, at least under certain circumstances, such as a war emergency. There are also a number of ways to increase the productivity of labor, for example, through stimulating research and the application of research, education, and so on. But the immediate answers to the domestic problems of inflation and unemployment usually lie in influencing planned spending and actual GNP rather than potential GNP.

Planned Spending and the Balance of Payments

Changes in planned spending also have important effects on the nation's balance of international payments. A nation's balance of payments during any period (usually a year) is essentially the difference between its spending abroad and its receipts from abroad. Such spending and receipts may arise from imports and exports of goods and services (the current account) or financial transactions —loans and investments (the capital account).

If a nation spends more abroad than it receives from abroad, it is said to have a *deficit* in its balance of payments.[4] A *surplus* in the

---

[4] There has been considerable discussion about how to measure a nation's balance-of-payments deficit (or surplus). The basic issue involves whether to in-

balance of payments occurs when receipts in the current and capital accounts exceed expenditures.

A balance-of-payments deficit in one year or a few years is not necessarily a cause for alarm. However, if a nation shows a persistent tendency toward a balance-of-payments deficit (or surplus), the disequilibrium will cause a problem. A persistent deficit by the United States, for example, results in the accumulation of dollars by foreigners (in the form of official holdings of deposits in U.S. banks or other short-term assets, such as Treasury bills) as our payments (of dollars) to them exceed our receipts (of dollars) from them. To the extent that foreign monetary authorities do not wish to hold such accumulations of dollars, they are likely to purchase gold from the United States, thereby reducing U.S. gold reserves.

If the rate of exchange between dollars and other currencies were free to move with market pressures, a persistent deficit would cause the dollar to depreciate—the accumulation of dollars by foreigners would permit them to offer more dollars for a unit of some other currency and the value of the dollar in terms of other currencies would fall. However, exchange rates between currencies do not move freely but are pegged—that is, fixed by official policy. The United States accomplishes this by fixing the dollar price (to foreigners) of gold—at $35 per ounce—while foreign governments similarly fix the price of gold (or dollars) in terms of their currencies.

When a country shows a persistent deficit in its balance of payments, the pegged exchange rate can be maintained, in the short run, by the use of foreign exchange and gold reserves to buy back the country's currency and keep its price at the pegged level. Other countries or international organizations may lend the deficit country the needed gold or currencies to preserve its exchange rate if the ultimate result of such action seems likely to be the restoration of a

---

clude certain short-term loans and investments in the capital account. Since the deficit or surplus in the balance of payments is the sum of the deficits (surpluses) in the current and capital accounts, inclusion or exclusion of certain transactions obviously has a noticeable effect on the size of the overall deficit or surplus. For a discussion of these issues, see U.S. Review Committee for Balance of Payments Statistics, *The Balance of Payments Statistics of the United States: A Review and Appraisal,* Report to the Bureau of the Budget (1965). Here we shall put all short-term *private* capital movements in the capital accounts, that is, we shall adopt the "official transactions" definition of the deficit in the balance of payments.

balance. Such short-run adjustments can continue only as long as a country's reserves of gold and foreign currencies last. The ultimate cure for a balance-of-payments deficit is to eliminate the deficit by reducing outlays abroad and increasing receipts from abroad. This may be done by allowing the exchange rate to fall or actually pushing it down ("devaluing the currency") as a policy action. If the value of the dollar were to fall (in terms of other currencies), for example, foreigners could get more dollars per unit of their currencies; U.S. residents could get fewer units of foreign currencies per dollar. This would make U.S. goods cheaper to foreigners and foreign goods more expensive to U.S. buyers, thus increasing U.S. exports and decreasing U.S. imports and, in the process, tending to eliminate the deficit in the balance of payments.[5]

Except as a last resort (such as the United Kingdom devaluations in 1949 and 1967), this solution is ruled out under present world monetary arrangements—a deficit country must instead find means to reduce spending abroad (imports of goods and services, loans, and investments) and/or increase receipts from abroad (exports of goods and services, loans, and investments). One means of reducing a deficit is to restrain or reduce total planned spending of businesses, consumers, and government. Imports of goods and services depend in part on total income (spending) of domestic sectors. Reducing aggregate domestic spending thus reduces imports and, through a reduction in the current account, the balance-of-payments deficit.

Federal Budget Policy and Planned Spending

The federal government can exert considerable influence on spending and thus on prices, employment, output, and the balance of payments by adjusting its expenditures or taxes—that is, by its use of fiscal policy.[6]

[5] This result is not assured, however. It depends basically on the price-responsiveness of the supply of and demand for exported and imported goods.

[6] The responsibility for fiscal policy in the United States lies with the federal government. Although all levels of government—federal, state, and local—engage in making budgets and thus are engaged in budget policy, only the federal government is large enough for its budgetary decisions to have an extensive impact on the whole economy. In addition, it is difficult for a state or local government

The Use of Fiscal Policy

The federal government affects planned spending by changing its own spending on goods and services and by causing consumer and business spending on goods and services to change by affecting consumer and business income. First, what causes private spending to change?

Private planned spending is affected by several factors. One of these, which receives particular emphasis at the working level of public policy, is the relation of private spending to private disposable income. Private disposable income is the income that is available for spending on goods and services by consumers and business firms after taxes and other deductions. Consumer spending varies directly with disposable income, that is, the higher disposable income is, all other things being equal, the higher consumer spending will be, and the lower disposable income is, the lower consumer spending will be. Likewise, the higher business income is, the higher investment by business can be expected to be, all other things being the same. In fact, businessmen often speak of the need for higher retained earnings for larger volumes of investment.

However, businesses and consumers do not spend all of any increase in their incomes but save part of it. And when their incomes fall their spending does not fall by the same amount. Thus private spending does rise and fall when private disposable income changes, but not proportionately.

Private spending is also affected by other forces, in particular by the liquidity of businesses and households,[7] terms of lending or credit conditions, and expectations concerning future income and prices. When expectations change, when credit conditions or terms of lending change, or when the liquidity of businesses and house-

---

alone to pursue a policy designed to affect employment or prices, since neighboring states or localities may pursue opposite policies and frustrate its efforts.

Since interest in this chapter is in federal fiscal policy—how the federal budget affects the economy—the budget referred to is the *national income budget,* which (1) includes receipts and expenditures of trust funds, such as OASI and the highway trust funds, (2) excludes purely credit transactions, and (3) generally treats tax receipts on an accrual basis and expenditures on a delivery basis.

[7] Liquidity is a measure of the extent to which consumers' and businesses' incomes are cash or assets readily convertible to cash.

holds is affected, planned spending for all levels of private disposable income is affected. For example, if businesses and consumers suddenly become more optimistic about future expectations, they will plan to spend more of their disposable income. If they become pessimistic, they will plan to spend less. If firms' and consumers' holdings become more liquid, perhaps because of an increase in their cash holdings, their spending will increase at all levels of disposable income, and if they become less liquid, their spending will decrease. Finally, if credit gets tight or interest rates rise, private planned spending at all levels of disposable income can be expected to fall, and the opposite relationship also holds.

Suppose expectations, liquidity, and credit conditions are given. How can federal budget action affect private planned spending? It can do so by changing the level of private disposable income. If the federal government reduces the amount it takes out of the GNP in taxes, consumers and businesses will be left with larger disposable incomes. This will encourage more private spending, both on domestically produced goods and imports, and GNP and imports will rise. By contrast, if the federal government increases taxes, this will reduce disposable income, reduce private spending, and cause GNP and imports to fall. Alternatively, the federal government can affect private disposable income by changes in federal spending on goods and services. Increased federal spending results in added income for someone. The industries receiving orders for federal goods have greater profits and pay more wages to their labor forces. With more income, businesses and consumers spend more.

Thus the federal government can affect private spending by changing private disposable income—either by changing taxes or by changing federal spending, which eventually changes private incomes. The precise effects of these changes and combinations of the two will be considered below.

Effects of Changes in Federal Spending

Suppose the federal government decreases its purchases of goods and services without changing tax rates. What will the effect of this be on the economy?

Other things being equal, decreased expenditures by the federal government have a contractionary effect. That is, they tend to lower output and employment and, at the same time, improve the balance of payments by causing imports to fall. Increases in government purchases, on the other hand, have an expansionary effect. In the discussion of how GNP is calculated, it was pointed out that GNP reflects planned spending. It was also pointed out that imports vary in the same direction as planned spending. Clearly, if government spending is increased, total planned spending, imports, GNP, and employment will increase (or if the economy is already at full employment, prices and wages will rise).

Suppose that GNP is $800 billion and is equal to planned spending, so that there is no tendency for it to change. Suppose also that consumers and businesses together spend 65 percent of any increase in private disposable income—60 on domestic goods and 5 on imported goods; that is, each $1 change in private disposable income changes consumption and investment (including imports of goods) by 65 cents. Finally, suppose that government taxes away 20 percent of any increase in GNP, the federal budget is balanced, and there is no deficit or surplus in the balance of payments. Now, what will be the effect on GNP and the balance of payments if federal purchases of goods and services are permanently decreased by $10 billion? (This decrease might result from a reduction in purchases of missiles or submarines, construction of new government buildings, or the number of government employees.) The decrease in total government spending by $10 billion will, in this example, cause output to fall by $19.2 billion, or almost twice the decrease in government spending. At the same time, a surplus of almost $1 billion will arise in the balance of payments.

Why is this the case? Why does a decrease in government spending cause a multiple decrease in output and improve the balance of payments? The answer is basically very simple. When the government spends $10 billion less (and keeps its spending at the new lower level), GNP, or output, will first fall by the amount (assuming it would have been spent domestically) of goods and services, or output, the government would have purchased. However, as the $10 billion of income is lost by consumers and business firms, they will reduce expenditures on investment and consumption, and GNP will fall further. Under the assumptions we have made, out of each dollar of income lost as purchases fall, 20 cents will represent the reduction in taxes paid; after-tax incomes will fall by 80 cents. Consumers and firms will thus reduce their spending on domestic goods by 48 cents (that is, 60 percent of 80 cents). So each dollar of income lost will, according to our assumption, reduce private domestic spending by 48 cents. GNP will fall initially by $10 billion because of the decrease in government purchases; the loss in income will induce a fall in private domestic spending of $4.8 billion. This fall in spending will reduce income still further, which will in turn reduce private domestic spending by an additional $2.3 billion (60 percent of $3.8 billion, the fall in private disposable income after allowing for the $1 billion fall in taxes paid), and so on until a total

FIGURE 11. Effect on GNP of a $10 Billion Decrease in Federal Purchases

Billions of dollars

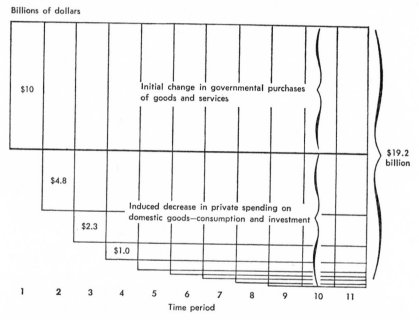

change in GNP of $19.2 billion is reached, as shown in Figure 11: $10 billion less of government purchases of goods and services and $9.2 billion less of private spending on domestic goods. At the same time output of domestic goods is reduced, purchases of imports are also reduced; 5 percent of each decrease in disposable income is reflected in a reduction in imports. Imports will thus fall by $768 million.

The whole process is reversed when there is an increase in government purchases of goods and services. This causes GNP to rise by 1.92 times the increase in government purchases of goods and services and imports to rise by 5 percent of the increase in GNP.

One qualification needs to be made at this point. The net contractionary effects of a permanent decrease in government spending may be reduced if private or state and local government expenditures are substituted for those that would otherwise have been undertaken. If, for example, the government has been absorbing investment opportunities open to the private sector, private investment outlays will rise when government spending falls, and this will counteract the restrictive effect of the decrease. The effect will also be reduced if part or all of the decrease in government purchases is in the area of imported goods and services. In this case, the direct effect of the decrease on domestic output will be reduced by the amount that would have been spent on foreign goods, and thus the multiplier effect of a decrease in expenditures will also be reduced. In the example given above it is assumed that neither of these offsets is present.

So decreases in government spending on goods and services are generally contractionary, and increases have a stimulative effect. If there is slack in the economy, an increase in spending will cause output to rise. If the economy is already at full employment, an increase may bring about some increase in real output but most certainly will cause prices to rise. Increases in government spending tend to increase imports by causing total planned spending to rise, thus increasing the deficit (or decreasing the surplus) in the balance of payments; decreases tend to improve the balance of payments.

Effects of Changes in Federal Taxes

Assuming that everything else (including government expenditures) remains the same, an increase in federal tax rates on incomes will increase tax revenues at any level of GNP, and a decrease will reduce tax revenues. An increase in tax revenues means less private disposable income, and this in turn means, all other things being equal, less private spending. So whatever the level of GNP, a tax increase will tend to reduce output (GNP) and imports because it will reduce private spending. A tax cut, on the other hand, will tend to raise output and imports by raising private spending.[8]

___

[8] Changes in certain types of government expenditures have the same effect on GNP as tax changes in that they change private disposable income without chang-

Suppose the situation is the same as in the example given above of the effects of a government spending decrease (pp. 72–74). Suppose that, with GNP at $800 billion, the federal government decides to raise tax rates.[9] Specifically, suppose that a rise in tax rates is planned so that, if GNP stays at $800 billion, tax revenues will rise by $10 billion. This could be accomplished by raising the percentage of the change in GNP that is taken by taxes from 20 to 21¼; the higher rate would bring in $10 billion more revenue.

The effect of this $10 billion tax increase will be to cause the level of GNP to fall by $11.3 billion, or 1.13 times the tax increase of $10 billion. The process is similar to that in the case of the government expenditure decrease. The increase in taxes will initially take away $10 billion of disposable income from the private sector. This fall in disposable income will cause the private sector to spend $6 billion less on domestic goods (60 percent of $10 billion). The reduction in spending will generate a further fall in income of $6 billion, of which $4.72 billion constitutes a reduction in spending on domestic goods and about $1.28 billion a reduction in tax revenues.[10] As private spending is reduced by $4.72 billion, income will fall by the same amount. This fall in income will be reflected in another reduction in spending by the private sector: 60 percent of $4.72 billion, or $2.83 billion. Income will again automatically fall by an equal amount, and the process will be repeated until the total decrease of $11.3 billion has been reached.

---

ing government purchases of goods and services. The most important of these at the federal level are interest payments on the federal debt and so-called transfer payments. The latter consist of payments made to individuals where no service is rendered, such as unemployment compensation and old-age benefits. Decreases in transfer payments or (net) interest payments are comparable to increases in taxes, since they also reduce private disposable income. Increases in transfer payments or (net) interest payments have the same effect as tax cuts; that is, they increase private disposable income.

Hence, throughout our discussion in this chapter we use the terms "expenditure changes" loosely to mean changes in purchases of goods and services and "tax changes" to mean changes in transfer and interest payments as well as tax changes narrowly defined.

[9] The focus will be on changes in tax *rates,* since this is the more common way of changing taxes. We could have used changes in exemptions; they work somewhat differently, but the general effects are the same.

[10] Note that the change in taxes per dollar change in GNP is now 21¼ cents because the tax rate is now 21¼ percent instead of 20 percent. Clearly, the effects of changes in tax rates on GNP will be different for different rates.

The fall in private incomes will also cause imports to fall, thus improving the balance of payments—increasing the surplus or reducing the deficit. However, the decrease in imports will not be large in this case since the fall in GNP was not large.

Note that although a tax increase of $10 billion was assumed, actual tax revenues will not rise by this amount. The $10 billion increase was based on the old level of GNP ($800 billion). But since the tax increase will have a contractionary effect and cause GNP to fall, the increase in revenue will be partially offset by the fall in GNP. The fall in GNP of $11.3 billion will induce a fall in tax receipts of 21¼ percent of the change in GNP, or some $2.4 billion. The net effect on the budget deficit will be to decrease it not by $10 billion but by only $7.6 billion.

This discrepancy will also occur in the case of the government expenditure decrease mentioned earlier. Because the reduction will induce a fall in GNP, tax revenues will also fall. The fall in GNP will cause tax revenues to fall by an amount equal to $3.84 billion (that is, 20 percent of the $19.2 billion decrease in GNP), which will be a partial offset to the reduction in government expenditures of $10 billion, and the deficit will be reduced by only $6.16 billion.[11]

Achieving the Domestic Goal of Full Employment GNP
by Changing Expenditures and Taxes

It has been noted that decreases in government purchases of goods and services and increases in tax rates are both contractionary. Obviously, fiscal policy measures can combine tax and expendi-

---

[11] This analysis of the effects of expenditures and taxes on GNP and the balance of payments ignores the effects on spending of changes in money or other assets held by the public as a result of deficits or surpluses in the government budget. As long as the government runs a deficit, net assets held by the public (money or government securities) will increase, and this will tend to raise private spending apart from the effects on income of tax and expenditure changes. The relationship holds in the opposite direction as well: as long as the government runs a surplus, there will be a downward pressure on private demand apart from changes in income. When the effects of a deficit or surplus on private spending are taken into account, the tax and expenditure multipliers are found to be larger than the analysis in this chapter suggests. For a more complete discussion of this point, see David J. and Attiat F. Ott, "Budget Balance and Equilibrium Income," *Journal of Finance*, March 1965, pp. 71–77, and Wallace E. Oates, "Budget Balance and Equilibrium Income: A Comment on the Efficacy of Fiscal and Monetary Policy in an Open Economy," *Journal of Finance*, September 1966, pp. 489–98.

ture changes to achieve the domestic goal of making actual GNP equal to full employment GNP.

Assume that the economy is in an inflationary period where total spending is excessive; actual output is greater than full employment output (at current prices); and there is upward pressure on prices. Under these conditions, five combinations of tax and expenditure changes can be used to attain the objective of matching planned spending and full employment output:

1. The federal government can decrease its purchases of goods and services without changing tax rates.

2. The federal government can increase tax rates without changing its purchases.

3. The federal government can simultaneously decrease spending and raise tax rates, thus using both tools to lower GNP.

4. The federal government can decrease both spending and taxes.

5. The federal government can raise spending and increase taxes, as long as the tax increase is sufficiently greater than the rise in government spending.

To illustrate some of these possibilities, we will use our earlier example, where GNP was $800 billion. Suppose that GNP (measured at current prices) is $50 billion greater than full employment GNP (also measured at current prices), which is $750 billion. How large a decrease in government spending will it take to lower GNP by $50 billion? Under the assumptions we made earlier about the percentage change in income spent and the additional percentage of GNP taken by taxes, for every dollar of decrease in government spending, GNP will tend to fall by $1.92. If GNP is to fall by $50 billion, then, by a change in government spending alone, the required change can be obtained by dividing $50 billion by 1.92. The result is $26 billion. This method of reducing GNP will increase the surplus or reduce the deficit by $16 billion. The fall of $50 billion in GNP will reduce tax revenue by $10 billion (20 percent of $50 billion), which will partially offset the decrease of $26 billion in expenditures.

Now suppose that, under the same conditions, the federal government attempts to reduce GNP by $50 billion by increasing tax rates alone. The necessary dollar tax increase, at the old GNP level, can be arrived at by dividing $50 billion by 1.13 (the tax multiplier) to obtain $44.2 billion. At the old GNP of $800 billion, this would mean an increase in tax rates from 20 percent to 24.3 percent of the change in GNP, or by 4.3 percentage points.[12] The effect on the government's budget position in this case would be to increase the surplus or reduce the deficit by $32.0 billion; the $44.2 billion rise in taxes would be offset partially by a $12.2 billion fall in taxes (24.3 percent of $50 billion) resulting from the decrease in GNP of $50 billion.

Thus, to achieve the same reduction in GNP, the required tax increase would be larger (in dollar terms) than the required cut in government purchases of goods and services. This is consistent with our earlier analysis of the effects of tax and expenditure changes, where a change in government purchases was seen to affect GNP more than an equal dollar change in taxes. It should also be noted that, because a larger tax increase would be required to achieve the same change in GNP, the tax increase would have a greater impact on the surplus or deficit of the government. The decrease in government purchases would increase the surplus or reduce the deficit by $16 billion, whereas the tax increase achieving the same reduction in GNP would increase the surplus or reduce the deficit by $32.0 billion.

The government can also close the gap between actual and full employment GNP by policies combining in various ways decreases in purchases of goods and services and increases in taxes. For example, if, to achieve a decrease in GNP of $50 billion, it were decided to decrease government purchases of goods and services by $10 billion, this alone would reduce GNP by about $19.2 billion, and the tax increase needed to produce the remaining $30.8 billion decrease in GNP could easily be calculated.[13] Similarly, other combinations of taxes and purchases can be used to accomplish a $50 billion reduction in GNP, ranging from a zero decrease in government purchases at one extreme to a $26 billion decrease at the other. These are the limits of possible changes. At one extreme, only taxes are increased with zero change in government purchases, and, at the other, only government purchases are increased, by $26 billion

---

[12] Again note that the tax multiplier differs depending on the tax *rate* needed to obtain the desired change in GNP.

[13] In this case it would be 27.3 billion ($30.8 billion divided by 1.13).

(since the government purchases multiplier is equal to 1.92), with no change in taxes. Thus the effect on the surplus or deficit, depending on the combination chosen, will be somewhere between $16 billion and $32.0 billion.

Finally, it should be clear that GNP can be reduced by cutting government purchases and taxes equally, that is, by balanced reductions in government purchases and taxes. If a dollar change in government purchases affects GNP more than a dollar change in taxes, then clearly a decrease of $1 in government purchases will decrease GNP more than a $1 decrease in taxes will raise GNP. That is, although decreased spending by government lowers GNP and decreased taxes raise GNP, the expenditure change has more impact than the tax change, and so, on balance, GNP will fall when government expenditures and taxes are reduced equally. Thus, equal reductions in government spending and taxes can be planned to close the gap between actual GNP and full employment GNP. In short, balanced budget changes are not inconsistent with the use of expenditure and tax policy to maintain full employment and price stability.

As has been implied, equal decreases in government purchases and taxes will have much less impact than changes in government purchases alone. So when actual GNP is above full employment GNP, smaller surpluses will be incurred if full employment is maintained through expenditure decreases rather than through tax increases.

The example given above dealt with an inflationary situation. The opposite case could just as well have been chosen, where planned spending at full employment GNP is below output (at current prices), that is, where there is a tendency toward unemployment and excess capacity. The objective then would be to increase planned spending. This could be done by increasing government purchases, or by reducing taxes, or by increasing government purchases *and* reducing taxes, or by increasing both government purchases and taxes. All the conclusions reached concerning the necessary changes in government purchases and taxes in each case and the effects on the budget would simply be reversed in this situation.

It should be recognized that, in actual practice, the effects of tax and expenditure policy might not work out exactly as described here. There might be changes in expectations or some other circumstance that would cause the relation of spending and income to vary and thus alter the final outcome. This discussion has assumed that "all other things have been equal."

Achieving Balance-of-Payments Equilibrium by Changing Expenditures and Taxes

From our discussion of the relation between planned spending and the balance of payments and our discussion of the effects of tax or expenditure changes on planned spending, it is obvious that fiscal policy measures can also be used to achieve the external goal of balance-of-payments equilibrium. An expansionary fiscal policy (a combination of tax and expenditure changes which increases planned spending) increases the deficit in a nation's balance of payments (or reduces the surplus) by increasing imports. A restrictive fiscal policy (one which reduces planned spending) improves the balance of payments (reduces the deficit or increases the surplus) by reducing imports.

In certain situations the appropriate fiscal policy for achieving domestic goals is inconsistent with that for achieving balance-of-payments equilibrium. In other situations, both objectives can be achieved with the same direction in fiscal policy. There are, in fact, four possible situations; in two there is no conflict between the two goals and the appropriate direction of fiscal policy, and in the other two such conflict does exist. These four possibilities are shown in Table 10.

The United States was characterized by situation 2 during much of the 1950's and by situation 4 during most of the period 1960–65.

Table 10. Appropriate Direction of Fiscal Policy under Different Economic Circumstances

	Appropriate fiscal policy for each goal	
Economic situation	Full employment and price stability	Balance-of-payments equilibrium
1. Domestic inflation and deficit in balance of payments	Restrictive	Restrictive
2. Unemployment and surplus in balance of payments	Expansionary	Expansionary
3. Domestic inflation and surplus in balance of payments	Restrictive	Expansionary
4. Unemployment and balance-of-payments deficit	Expansionary	Restrictive

Thus during the latter period, fiscal policy alone could not move us toward both our internal and external objectives. In 1966 and early 1967, however, situation 1 developed, and restrictive fiscal action was called for to achieve both our internal and external goals.

It should be noted that fiscal policy is not quite as helpless to achieve both goals simultaneously as situations 3 and 4 suggest. We have developed our analysis of the balance-of-payments effects of fiscal actions only in terms of the effects of general tax or expenditure changes on imports. It is possible to use a combination of fiscal actions to stimulate domestic spending while avoiding a worsening of the balance of payments or to restrain spending without also reducing imports. Specific taxes can be levied on exports or imports, or exports and imports may be subsidized in spending programs. Taxes may be levied to affect capital flows, as with the so-called interest equalization tax passed in 1964 and renewed in 1967, which places a special tax on the purchase of foreign securities by U.S. residents; or taxes may be levied on foreign travel by U.S. tourists, as proposed by President Johnson in early 1968.[14]

In general, though, fiscal policy cannot bear all of the burden of moving us toward both domestic and external economic objectives in all circumstances—it must be used in a proper combination with *monetary policy*. In fact, fiscal policy may not work at all as we have pictured it here without assistance from monetary policy. How potent fiscal policy is in relation to monetary policy has become the subject of considerable debate among economists, with the outcome of crucial significance in determining the weight to be placed on tax and expenditure changes as a means to affect output, employment, prices, and the balance of payments.

The Limitations of Fiscal Policy

Our discussion of the effects of changes in government expenditures or taxes must certainly be qualified. Consider the case where

[14] Under the interest equalization tax, a tax of up to 15 percent is levied on securities purchased from nonresidents by U.S. residents. By thus making it more costly for foreigners to raise capital in the United States, the outflow of U.S. capital is discouraged.

President Johnson's proposal involved an excise tax on tickets purchased in the United States for travel outside the Western Hemisphere and a tax on expenditures of U.S. tourists while abroad (outside the Western Hemisphere).

GNP rises because government expenditures are increased or taxes are cut. If the rise in GNP is not accompanied by an increase in money or other liquid assets, individuals and firms will have fewer liquid assets relative to their incomes. They will try to obtain additional cash, or assets virtually as liquid as cash, by selling off their securities until they are satisfied with their liquidity position. It is generally believed that individuals and firms will accept a poorer liquidity position only at higher interest rates or yields. That is, individuals or firms will accept the greater risk of being caught with no cash, or assets readily convertible to cash, only if the risk is compensated by a higher return on their earning assets. If higher interest rates are required to induce the private sector to accept a poorer liquidity position, at least part of the expansive effect of increased government purchases or lower taxes will be offset by these higher rates. Private spending, particularly for residential construction and business investment in plant and equipment, is to some degree sensitive to interest rates. Businessmen will forego projects when the cost of borrowing approaches or exceeds the return on a project. Therefore, higher interest rates brought about by the efforts of firms and individuals to obtain an acceptable liquidity position will have some restraining effect on private spending, thus offsetting in part the expansive effect of the tax cut or expenditure increase. In short, the multiplier effect of tax or expenditure changes will be smaller because of the concomitant effects on liquidity and interest rates.

How much the impact of government fiscal policy is reduced by higher interest rates depends on (1) the relation between interest rates and the desired liquidity positions of firms and individuals and (2) the relation between interest rate changes and changes in private spending. The less responsive the public's demand for money and other liquid assets is to interest rates, the higher the interest rates must rise when GNP rises (assuming the stock of money does not change or that it increases less than the demand for it) to induce the public to accept a worsened liquidity position. Thus, any tax or expenditure change which causes GNP to rise will (initially) have this offsetting effect. And the more responsive private spending is to interest rate changes, the greater the offsetting effect of any given interest rate rise on private expenditures. In short, the less responsive the demand for liquid assets and the more responsive private expenditures are to interest rate changes, the less effective fiscal policy will be in affecting planned spending, unemployment, prices, and the balance of payments.

In recent years, one school of economists has argued vigorously that, in fact, fiscal policy has very little to do with planned spending and output because the demand for money and other liquid assets is not very sensitive to interest rates whereas private expenditures are. In this view, the only significant effects of fiscal policy on GNP occur as a result of changes in the stock of money and other liquid assets which avoid the effects of higher interest rates that would otherwise block most of the direct impact of tax and expenditure changes. This school of thought is most closely identified with Professor Milton Friedman of the University of Chicago,[15] who argues that it is substantial changes in the stock of money over short periods that have been a major factor in changes in spending and the level of business activity, employment, and prices, at least in the final analysis.[16] In short, this school maintains that fiscal actions are of little consequence for output, prices, unemployment, and the balance of payments, whereas monetary policy—defined as changes in the rate of growth of the money supply—is of major importance.

This view has received considerable attention in light of difficulties with inflationary pressures experienced during 1965 and 1966.[17] The "money school" attributes the rapid expansion of 1961–65, the inflation of mid-1965 to late 1966, and the slowdown in the economy in early 1967, not to fiscal measures, but to the rate

[15] For a very readable and concise exposition of Friedman's views on fiscal policy, see his *Capitalism and Freedom* (University of Chicago Press, 1962), pp. 79–84.

[16] This view is set forth most clearly, perhaps, in his report on work in monetary research to the National Bureau of Economic Research; see National Bureau of Economic Research, *Forty-fourth Annual Report,* June 1964, pp. 10–25. See esp. p. 20, where he seeks to differentiate his findings from what are often fallacious popular versions of them. Friedman explicitly points out that he does *not* say "the growth of the money supply is the single most important factor affecting the nation's economy" (p. 20).

[17] See *Business Week,* May 13, 1967, pp. 96–98, and April 15, 1967, pp. 188–92, for discussion of two debates over economic policy held in Washington during the spring of 1967 which reflect the attention being given the "money school." The intensity of the debate was also brought out in a column in the *Washington Post,* April 16, 1967, by James Tobin, a member of the Council of Economic Advisers under President Kennedy. In the article Tobin mounts a direct attack, aimed for popular consumption, on the money school.

of growth in the money supply provided by the Federal Reserve. The rate of change of the money stock is, in fact, a leading indicator of the level of business activity.[18]

The defenders of the potency of fiscal policy criticize the money school largely on the ground that a link from money to spending to economic activity is in no way implied by the relation between the rate of change of money and the level of output or business activity.[19] They argue that "most likely, money and business activity are both the results of a complex economic process" and that, without a clear explanation of why the relationship exists, the relationship alone does not prove that money is a major factor in the ups and downs of the economy and that fiscal policy is not.[20] They point to the fiscal policy actions they believe were of crucial importance in producing the expansions of 1960–65, namely, an increase of $32 billion in federal expenditures and a reduction of $16 billion in net tax receipts (measured at full employment GNP).[21] They argue further that failure to exercise fiscal restraint in early 1966 (by cutting nondefense expenditures or raising taxes) in the face of a $5 billion rise in the rate of defense spending between mid-1965 and early 1966 played a major role in the 1966 inflation.[22] In short, while not denying the independent and important effects monetary policy has on the economy, the defenders of fiscal policy argue that fiscal actions as well contributed to the economic achievements and disappointments of the 1960–67 period and that, in conjunction, fiscal and monetary policy can exert a powerful influence over business activity.

The importance of the issues raised in this debate is obvious. If

[18] For a succinct statement of this thesis, see Milton Friedman's column in *Newsweek,* Oct. 17, 1966, p. 92. Changes in the rate of growth of the money supply form a series whose behavior corresponds to but precedes changes in business activity published in the U.S. Department of Commerce's monthly publication *Business Cycle Indicators.*

[19] See Tobin, *Washington Post,* April 16, 1967, p. G-2.

[20] *Ibid.*

[21] The data are from Walter W. Heller, *New Dimensions of Political Economy* (W. W. Norton, 1967), p. 71. He, in turn, had revised the data presented by the Council of Economic Advisers in testimony before the Subcommittee on Fiscal Policy of the Joint Economic Committee in the summer of 1965; see *Fiscal Policy Issues of the Coming Decade,* Hearings before the Subcommittee on Fiscal Policy, Joint Economic Committee, 89 Cong. 1 sess. (1965), pp. 1–14.

[22] Heller, *New Dimensions of Political Economy,* pp. 85–99.

the money school is correct, primary emphasis must be placed on monetary policy to achieve the nation's objectives of full employment, price stability, and balance-of-payments equilibrium. If the views of the other group are correct, both fiscal and monetary policy have roles to play. These issues cannot be resolved here. To some extent answers will be obtained from the results of future empirical studies by economists; they may also evolve from the results of actual attempts to apply one view or the other. We take the position that fiscal policy actions—changes in expenditures or taxes—do have significant effects on planned spending, and in the next section we will investigate how fiscal policy may be used, together with monetary policy, to achieve our internal and external economic objectives.

The Appropriate Mix of Fiscal and Monetary Policy

By buying or selling government securities (open market operations), the Federal Reserve System can affect interest rates and, through interest rates, planned spending (particularly housing investment and to a lesser degree business spending on inventories and plant and equipment).[23] Thus, monetary policy initiated by the Federal Reserve System affects output, prices, employment, and the balance of payments through its effect on planned spending, as fiscal policy does.

However, monetary policy exerts an influence on the balance-of-payments deficit or surplus apart from its effect on planned spending and imports (the current account). The level of interest rates in the United States vis à vis those abroad affects capital movements—our loans and investments abroad and the flow of foreign funds to the United States. This is particularly true for short-term capital flows and may also be true for flows of long-term capital for portfolio investments. Thus a rise in U.S. interest rates resulting from a more restrictive monetary policy tends to attract foreign funds to the United States and discourage outflows of U.S. funds, and a decrease

[23] This is not to say that the *only* effects of monetary policy on planned spending occur through changes in interest rates or that the level of interest rates is necessarily the proper target of monetary policy or an indicator of the "ease" or "tightness" of monetary policy. It is useful in this context, however, to equate monetary policy with determining the level of interest rates and to assume that the major effects of monetary policy occur through interest rate changes.

in interest rates has the opposite effect. In short, monetary policy, by affecting domestic interest rates, affects both the current account, by changing total planned spending and imports, *and* the capital account, by changing interest rate differentials between the United States and foreign countries.

For every level of interest rates a monetary authority might choose, there is some degree of fiscal ease or restraint that will make planned spending equal output and, assuming no "tradeoff problem," that will produce full employment and price stability. Further, for every level of interest rates, there is a degree of fiscal ease or restraint that will produce balance-of-payments equilibrium (a tendency for the balance-of-payments deficit to be zero). There are, in short, various monetary and fiscal policies which will achieve the nation's internal and external objectives, taken separately. The problem is to find that mixture of the two policies that simultaneously will achieve full employment, price stability, and balance-of-payments equilibrium. The proper pairing of policies and goals must be determined: Should fiscal policy be directed toward the domestic goals or the balance of payments? Toward which of the two goals should monetary policy be directed?

The importance of the proper pairing of fiscal and monetary policy and internal and external goals may be illustrated rather simply. Suppose the United States—with a certain combination of tax rates, government expenditures, and interest rates—has full employment but a balance-of-payments deficit. Should monetary or fiscal policy be used to eliminate the deficit? Suppose either a rise of 2 percentage points in interest rates or a $10 billion tax increase would (taken alone) eliminate the deficit, with the former causing GNP to fall by $8 billion and the latter causing it to fall by $12 billion. Clearly, in this situation we should use monetary policy to close the payments gap since it would give us a substantially greater effect per dollar of change in GNP than the fiscal policy remedy of a tax increase. In other words, fiscal or monetary policy should be directed toward the goal where it will have its greatest relative impact. In the example above, the $8 billion fall in GNP could be eliminated by a tax *cut*, the resulting increase in the deficit could be offset by a further rise in interest rates, and so on until both goals were achieved.

To repeat, the proper mixture of monetary and fiscal policy depends on the relative impact of each on GNP and the balance of payments. There has been some theoretical analysis of the problem which suggests that monetary policy should be directed toward the balance of payments while fiscal policy should be directed toward internal goals.[24] The basis of the conclusion could be the observation made earlier that monetary policy affects both the current and the capital accounts in the balance of payments, which suggests that the impact of monetary policy is much stronger on the balance of payments relative to GNP than the impact of fiscal policy. However, the issue is basically an empirical one; and no pairing of policies and goals is indisputably correct given the present state of knowledge. What is clear is that fiscal and monetary policy cannot be mixed indiscriminately unless the relative impact of each on the balance of payments and GNP is the same, which is a very restrictive condition.

Restraints on Expenditure and Tax Changes

The economic impact of changes in federal spending and in taxes has been described, as well as the ways in which they can be used to combat unemployment and idle capacity, excess demand that results in inflation, or balance-of-payments disequilibrium. What mixture of expenditure and tax policy is appropriate? The problem of determining the proper mixture of monetary and fiscal policy has also been discussed. We will now look briefly at some of the practical problems in the use of expenditure or tax changes.

In the case of both these areas of fiscal policy—changes in government purchases of goods and services and tax rate changes— there are time lags that must be considered. There is the *recognition lag*—the time between the occurrence of an economic event (say, the beginning of a recession) and its observation and verification. Fiscal policy makers have various indicators at hand to check the health of the economy, such as the quarterly GNP estimates, the

---

[24] See Robert A. Mundell, "The Appropriate Use of Monetary and Fiscal Policy for Internal and External Stability," in International Monetary Fund, *Staff Papers* (March 1962), pp. 70–79. It is also possible to show that the proper pairing of fiscal and monetary policy is not obvious on purely theoretical grounds, since the relative impact of either monetary or fiscal policy on GNP and the balance of payments cannot be established a priori; see David J. Ott and Attiat F. Ott, "Monetary and Fiscal Policy: Goals and the Choice of Instruments," *Quarterly Journal of Economics,* May 1968, pp. 313–25.

monthly price index for consumer and wholesale goods, monthly unemployment data, and a wide variety of "leading," "coincident," and "lagging" indicators issued by the Department of Commerce. Ideally it would be desirable for fiscal authorities to be able to predict future changes in output, prices, unemployment, or the balance of payments that will require corrective action, but in the present state of knowledge all they usually can do is try to correct undesirable movements that are already under way.

There is also a lag between the recognition of an economic condition which requires action and the action itself. This is termed the *administrative lag*. The speed with which policies may be changed is determined by political as well as some technical considerations. The political aspects make the lag shorter for expenditure changes than for taxes, and the technical considerations work in the opposite direction. Although changes in appropriations and tax rates, exemptions, and brackets must be legislated by Congress, the President can to a limited extent vary the rate of expenditure during a given period through apportionment of appropriations by the Bureau of the Budget, as we have seen previously (Chapter 3). On the other hand, a given legislated change in tax policy may be put into effect much faster than an expenditure change. The effect of changing rates, brackets, or exemptions on private income is immediate, because of the withholding tax system for individuals and because taxes are computed on an accrual basis by corporations. The effect of expenditure programs is not felt as quickly for a number of reasons. In the first place, it takes time to plan the projects on which public funds will be spent. Second, even if the plans are already at hand, public projects cannot be put into operation at a moment's notice. There are many legal and institutional details, such as the letting of contracts and the procurement of materials, which must be accomplished before work can actually be undertaken. And once it is started, a public works or other antirecession program cannot be ended at will. Projects in progress have to be completed if they are to function or to avoid deterioration, even though the need for additional spending for stabilization purposes may no longer exist.

There is, finally, the *operational lag*. This is the time which elapses from the beginning of a policy change to the attainment of the desired results. On this count, tax changes are clearly more effective. When rates or exemptions are changed, the full effect occurs immediately and continues as long as the new policy is in effect.[25]

In general, both tax and expenditure changes are slow and somewhat clumsy instruments of policy, largely because of the need to obtain legislation from Congress for all significant policy changes. Discretionary fiscal action has been of very limited importance, for example, in reducing the severity or duration of postwar recessions because of its modest use and problems of timing.[26]

Presidents Kennedy and Johnson sought to improve the countercyclical powers of the government by asking Congress to give the President standby power to cut tax rates temporarily and to initiate public works programs to combat unemployment. Similar standby power to reduce taxes was proposed by the Commission on Money and Credit and the Committee for Economic Development. As was pointed out earlier, however, Congress has not granted any of these requests, apparently feeling that to do so would be an excessive delegation of its authority to the executive.

The Lewis study notes several factors that have prevented better use of discretionary fiscal action.[27] One can be described as "prior commitments and long-range goals." For example, President Truman, having just been elected to office in a campaign featuring charges of Republican "fiscal irresponsibility" because of the tax cut of 1948, was naturally reluctant to propose a tax cut in 1949 to combat that recession. Another factor of this kind has been the desire to maintain public and business confidence; policy makers have been reluctant to take discretionary fiscal action under certain conditions because such action would constitute explicit recognition of the existence of a recession and might have undesirable psychological effects. An impending need for sharp increases in defense outlays has made Presidents reluctant to take policy action in the early stages of recessions for fear of inflationary effects during recovery

[25] The money school argues that there are long and variable lags for both fiscal *and* monetary actions and in general opposes attempts to use discretionary policy of either sort to stabilize the economy. They favor instead the use of "rules," for example, a certain rate of growth in the money stock rather than discretionary action, on the grounds that, although monetary policy is more potent than fiscal policy, it works only with a considerable lag.

[26] See Wilfred Lewis, Jr., *Federal Fiscal Policy in the Postwar Recessions* (Brookings Institution, 1962).

[27] Lewis, *Federal Fiscal Policy in the Postwar Recessions,* p. 20.

periods. Public concern over budget deficits has also operated to limit the use of discretionary fiscal policy to combat a recession. And finally, emphasis on efficiency in the rate of expenditures has at times restrained action against recessions.

The time lags and other restraints on the use of discretionary tax and expenditure changes by the federal government have not had as serious effects as they might have had because of the automatic tax and expenditure changes (or their equivalent) that are built into the federal budget. These work to cushion the economy against recession and to restrain it during boom periods. How these *automatic fiscal stabilizers* can be properly combined with discretionary policy, and the resulting implications for the federal budget, are discussed below.

Automatic Fiscal Stabilizers

The automatic tax or expenditure changes built into the federal budget cushion private disposable income when GNP changes. By so doing, they moderate the fall of private spending when GNP falls and limit the increase in private spending when GNP rises. In addition GNP itself falls and rises less than it might otherwise because of their stabilizing effect. These stabilizers are automatic in the sense that they become effective when the level of GNP changes and do not require any decisions by the executive or Congress.

The two major fiscal stabilizers of the federal government are (1) transfer payments, which are paid by the federal government to the aged, the poor, the unemployed, and other needy people in the nation, and (2) taxes.

Transfer payments vary inversely with GNP; as GNP rises, they fall, and as GNP falls, they rise. For the most part, this is a reflection of the behavior of unemployment compensation, which rises when GNP falls (since unemployment increases) and falls when GNP rises. If, for example, a change in private spending causes GNP to fall, the effect of unemployment compensation payments will be to moderate the fall of private disposable income. And, as has already been seen, if the fall of disposable income is checked, the fall in GNP will also be moderated.

Our progressive tax structure also has a stabilizing effect. As income increases, the ratio of taxes to income increases. Personal exemptions of a specified amount of income from taxation do not lessen the progressive nature of the system since marginal rates increase as individuals move to higher brackets. Even if every dollar of income were taxed at the same rate—as long as individuals were allowed to exempt a given amount of income from taxation—the tax system would still be progressive, since GNP would have to reach a certain level before taxes would be paid at all. This by itself would mean that the ratio of taxes to GNP would rise as GNP rises, and vice versa, which is the definition of a progressive tax system.

The tax system is progressive also because marginal tax rates rise as one moves up to higher brackets. This means that the percentage of changes in GNP taken by taxes increases as GNP increases—as more people move up into higher tax brackets.

The importance of these automatic stabilizers in maintaining disposable personal income when GNP falls is clearly illustrated in Figure 12, which shows changes in GNP and disposable personal income by quarters for the period 1953–67. As can be seen, the fluctuations in disposable personal income were much smaller than those of GNP, and this is evidence of the operation of the automatic stabilizers.

FIGURE 12. Quarterly Changes in GNP and Disposable Income, 1953–67[a]

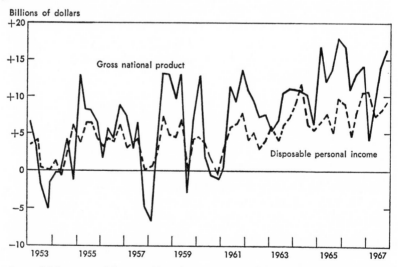

Sources: U.S. Department of Commerce, Office of Business Economics, *The National Income and Product Accounts of the United States, 1929–65* (1965), pp. 2–3, 34–35; and *Survey of Current Business*, 1967 and 1968 issues.
[a] Seasonally adjusted annual rates. Data for 1967 are preliminary.

The importance of the automatic stabilizers in the postwar period has been very great. Lewis found that "the built-in fiscal stabilizers have made a substantial contribution to the stability of the postwar economy."[28] Similarly, the Council of Economic Advisers, in its 1963 report, noted that "automatic fiscal stabilizers have made a major contribution in limiting the length and severity of postwar recessions."[29] However, it should be clearly understood that they act only to *stabilize* the economy, to prevent sharp upward and downward movements of GNP; they do not insure full employment GNP. If the economy were at full employment, and something brought about a decrease in planned private spending, the automatic fiscal stabilizers would reduce the impact on GNP of the fall in spending, but they would not reverse it. Discretionary action would be required to restore full employment GNP unless something else happened to restore private spending.

The Deficit or Surplus as a Measure of Fiscal Policy

Popular discussion of the effect of the budget on the economy— in the press, in Congress, and even to some extent among economists—often focuses on the current budget deficit or surplus. It is said that when the federal government runs a deficit, the effect on the economy is expansionary, and when it runs a surplus, the effect is restrictive.[30] As a matter of fact, the actual federal government surplus or deficit reveals nothing about the "tightness" or "looseness" of the government's fiscal program, and use of this as an indicator often leads to wrong conclusions.

The reason government deficits or surpluses are a poor guide for interpreting fiscal policy is that they reflect not only the decisions of Congress with regard to spending and tax rates (discretionary fiscal action) but also the response of tax revenues and transfer payments (the automatic stabilizers) to changes in GNP. Even with no change in tax rates or budgeted expenditures, the federal deficit or surplus varies as GNP varies. The federal deficit may increase because GNP falls (tax revenues fall, and transfer payments rise). Or

---

[28] *Ibid.*, p. 15.
[29] *Economic Report of the President, Together with the Annual Report of the Council of Economic Advisers* (1963), p. 67.
[30] Reference here is to a surplus or deficit in the national income budget.

Federal Budget Policy

FIGURE 13. Effect of Level of Economic Activity on Federal Surplus or Deficit

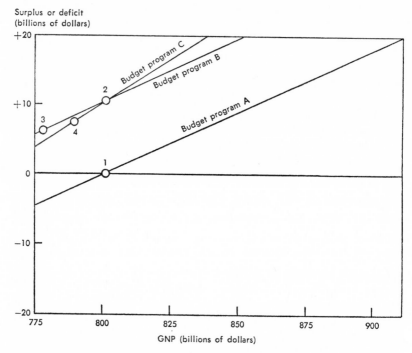

Source: Adapted from a graph developed by the Council of Economic Advisers in *Annual Report of the Council of Economic Advisers* (1962), pp. 78–80.

it may increase when GNP is rising, as a result of discretionary action—a tax cut or an increase in expenditures. The two components of the deficit are not the same in terms of their economic impact: one occurs as a result of a fall in GNP (and moderates that fall), while the other helps produce an increase in GNP. Since the impact in the two cases cannot be equated, the size of the federal deficit is clearly not a reliable measure of fiscal policy.

These distinctions may be made clearer with the aid of Figure 13, adapted from a graph developed by the Council of Economic Advisers in its 1962 report. The given budget or fiscal program (given tax rates and expenditures, except for transfer payments and others that vary with GNP) is indicated by the budget line labeled *A*. At any point on this line, the level of budgeted expenditures (those *not* varying with GNP) and tax rates are the same. The vertical axis measures the government's surplus or deficit (in the national income accounts budget); the horizontal axis measures the level of GNP. Since transfer payments fall and tax revenues increase as GNP rises, budget program *A* produces deficits at low levels of GNP, but as GNP rises, the deficit is reduced and turns into a surplus. This automatic change in the federal government's deficit or surplus resulting from changes in GNP, assuming a given fiscal program, is shown in the movement along budget line *A*.

An alternative fiscal program, with different tax rates or expenditures, will be reflected in a shift in the budget line.[31] Suppose that the fiscal program is modified by a tax increase or expenditure decrease, illustrated by line *B*. The surplus would be greater (the deficit less) at every level of GNP.

So the federal government's deficit or surplus in a particular period depends on two things: the fiscal program and the level of GNP. These two are not independent of one another, of course. The choice of a fiscal program will affect the level of GNP. If expenditures are decreased and the budget line *A* shifts upward, GNP will fall, as we have seen in our example on page 73. This example started with a balanced budget (point 1 in Figure 13). A $10 billion decrease in expenditures would shift the budget line up by $10 billion to line *B*, point 2. This would cause GNP to fall by almost $20 billion (point 3), making a net increase in the surplus of about $6 billion. A tax increase of $10 billion would shift the budget line up to *C*, point 2. This tax increase would produce a smaller reduction in GNP (point 4) and a larger increase in the surplus than would a reduction in expenditures.[32]

One further point deserves attention. The budget line will not always shift when there is a change in the fiscal program. Suppose government purchases and taxes are decreased equally for every level of GNP.[33] The budget line will not be affected because the effect of the decrease in government purchases on the deficit will be canceled out at every level of GNP by the decrease in taxes. But the

---

[31] This is not always the case, as will be noted below.

[32] Budget line *C* has a different slope than *A* or *B* because the percentage of change in GNP taken by taxes is changed. That is, an increase in this percentage by 1¼ points would increase the surplus by $10 billion at a GNP of $800 billion but would increase it by $11 billion at a GNP of $900 billion. So the budget line is steeper than before.

[33] In the case of taxes, this would approximately be achieved by changing exemption levels rather than marginal tax rates.

fiscal program has changed; the equal decrease in government purchases and taxes will, as we have seen, affect the level of GNP. So the budget line is not an unambiguous indicator of a fiscal program. It is simply a measure of the impact of different fiscal programs in terms of the surplus or deficit they produce at a given level of income. And as we have seen, the impact of fiscal policy is not measured by the surplus or deficit for a particular level of GNP but by the level of government purchases and taxes that produces the deficit or surplus. A surplus of $10 billion resulting from spending of $90 billion and tax revenues of $100 billion has a very different impact from a surplus of $10 billion resulting from spending of $190 billion and tax revenues of $200 billion.

In summary, the deficit or surplus that the federal government actually runs is no measure of the impact of fiscal policy because, first, it reflects both the automatic responses of taxes and transfers to changes in GNP and the discretionary changes in tax rates and spending. Second, it is not the deficit or surplus itself at any level of GNP (whether achieved or not) that is an adequate gauge of the impact of a fiscal program on the economy but the level of spending and taxes that produces the deficit or surplus.

Although the deficit or surplus does not provide a guide to fiscal action, it does involve certain implications for the proper use of fiscal policy to achieve budget balance, that is, to avoid the likelihood of continued deficits or surpluses. This is taken up in the next chapter.

Summary and Conclusions

This chapter has considered the general impact of federal spending and taxation within the framework of their effects on GNP. Decreases in government purchases of goods and services are contractionary, and decreases in tax rates (or increases in transfer payments) are expansionary; since imports vary with GNP, contractionary fiscal actions improve the balance of payments, and expansionary fiscal actions worsen the balance of payments. Changes in government spending on goods and services are more potent, per dollar, in their impact on GNP and the balance of payments than are changes in tax rates (or transfer payments).

The impact of fiscal actions on GNP and the balance of payments depends on the sensitivity to interest rates of the public's demand for liquid assets and private expenditures. The less responsive the public's demand for liquid assets and the more responsive private expenditures are to interest rate changes, the smaller the impact of changes in government expenditures or taxes. One school of thought—here called the "money school"—in fact argues that fiscal policy is relatively ineffective in changing output and the balance of payments, because the demand for liquid assets is insensitive to interest rate changes whereas private spending is highly sensitive to them. The adherents of this school feel that a more important major influence on GNP and the balance of payments is the rate of growth of the money supply. The "fiscal school," on the other hand, argues that both monetary and fiscal policy affect output and the balance of payments; monetary policy is an important consideration, but fiscal policy is not entirely impotent.

If budget policy and monetary policy both affect GNP and the balance of payments, they may be used together to achieve the domestic objectives of full employment and price stability and the external objective of balance-of-payments equilibrium. The proper combination of monetary and fiscal policy depends on the relative impact of each on GNP and the balance of payments; at present the evidence is not clear as to which policy should be paired with which goal.

The use of fiscal policy to make continuous adjustments in the economy is complicated by time lags in the execution and effect of expenditure and tax rate changes. However, the automatic fiscal stabilizers—the progressive personal income tax and transfer payments—smooth out fluctuations in GNP even though they cannot entirely eliminate them. The fact that the budget deficit or surplus reflects both the automatic responses of taxes and transfers to changes in GNP and the discretionary changes in tax rates and spending means that it cannot serve as an adequate measure of the impact of fiscal policy. Because expenditure and tax (or transfer payment) changes have different impacts, even the deficit or surplus measured at a given GNP level (such as full employment GNP) is not a meaningful measure of the impact of a fiscal program.

CHAPTER VI

Fiscal Policy and the Budget Program

By VARYING EITHER expenditures or taxes, or both, the federal government can work toward simultaneous low unemployment, price stability, and balance-of-payments equilibrium. By varying both in differing degrees and by combining these fiscal actions with the appropriate monetary policy, the federal government can achieve its goals and can do so with a balanced budget, a surplus, or a deficit. Given the role fiscal policy is to play, several questions now arise. What is the best combination of expenditures and taxes? Does this combination lead to deficits, surpluses, or a balanced budget? What reliance should be placed on the automatic fiscal stabilizers?

A Suggested Budget Policy

When discretionary fiscal policy is used, one very important consideration must be taken into account in deciding on the proper mix of changes in tax rates and in expenditures: that government expenditures and taxes play fundamentally different roles in the economy. When the government purchases goods and services, it is allocating resources between the public and private sectors according to the preferences of its citizens. This being so, it would seem that the allocation function of government expenditures should not be obscured by their use for fiscal policy reasons, that is, to affect the level of economic activity or the balance of payments. Expenditures should ideally be set at that level which—assuming full employment—achieves the public's desired allocation of resources between the production of public goods and private goods. If the public wants one-fifth of full employment output to go to defense, then expenditures should be set to produce this result. Or if it would rather have more automobiles and recreation, public expenditures should be adjusted accordingly.

Given the level of public expenditures that the people prefer—in terms of the allocation of resources—tax rates and transfers should generally be adjusted so as to produce the level of planned spending that will achieve the goal toward which fiscal policy is directed. Whether fiscal policy is directed toward the internal goal of full employment and price stability or toward the external goal of balance-of-payments equilibrium, the burden of adjusting total spending should fall mainly on taxes.

It should be recognized, however, that tax rate changes are not a perfect weapon for affecting planned spending. They may disrupt business planning and result in a deterioration of the tax system. Furthermore, in the current political situation, it is difficult to gain approval for a tax change, even though it might be the best means of achieving a goal.[1] If discretionary fiscal policy is to be used in the present setting, changes in government spending will have to be used along with tax rate changes.

What are the implications of this for budget balance? Basically, the important factor is private spending propensities. Once government expenditures are set, if private spending is high, then tax rates will have to be set high to avoid inflation or a balance-of-payments deficit, depending on which goal has been chosen by fiscal authorities. This combination of circumstances will tend to produce a budget surplus. On the other hand, if private spending is weak, tax

---

[1] The Revenue Act of 1964 has demonstrated that tax reduction can be effective in promoting higher incomes and employment. However, when inflationary pressures threaten, the experience of 1966 and 1967 has shown that it is much more difficult to get a tax increase approved by Congress. Although the latter is much less popular politically than tax cuts in periods of recession, there is no indication that the Congress is very receptive to either use of taxation for counter-cyclical purposes.

rates may have to be adjusted downward to achieve full employment output or to reduce the balance-of-payments surplus. If government expenditures are not changed, this may mean that a deficit must be run to achieve full employment. But it may also mean that a balanced budget will be consistent with full employment output without inflation or with equilibrium in the balance of payments.

Thus it seems obvious that the budget surplus or deficit is not the direct object of fiscal policy. Persistent deficits may be necessary to achieve full employment and balance-of-payments equilibrium, or it may be possible to achieve these goals and still balance the budget or even run a surplus. If fiscal policy is used properly (in conjunction with monetary policy), the level of taxes and expenditures will be set to achieve full employment without inflation and with balance-of-payments equilibrium and to achieve the desired allocation of resources. Surpluses or deficits will be allowed to occur where they may.

Although this general approach had the endorsement of the Johnson administration (and before it, the Kennedy administration), of important business and labor groups, and of expert bodies such as the Commission on Money and Credit, it has not been accepted by the general public. They have labeled it "fiscally irresponsible" to show so little interest in a balanced budget. In particular, the view that prolonged periods of weak private demand must produce sizable and perhaps persistent federal deficits, and thus a growing national debt, produces strong opposition that cuts across partisan lines.

The budget policy suggested here is one in which tax rates are adjusted, given a certain amount of government expenditures and the proper monetary policy, to produce full employment without inflation and balance-of-payments disequilibrium, with the help of automatic fiscal stabilizers to moderate the impact of short-run swings in business activity. This does not mean that tax rates should be continuously adjusted, however. In fact, they probably should not be varied too often, given the technical problem of estimating the magnitude of the needed rate change and the difficulty of securing changes from Congress. At times, changes in government spending may have to be used in place of, or as a complement to, changes in tax rates. The important points are that (1) discretionary fiscal policy should consist of tax rate changes as well as variations in expenditures; (2) tax rates should be set to achieve our economic objectives and not primarily to effect a change in the deficit or surplus; and (3) continued emphasis should be laid on automatic fiscal stabilizers for their cushioning effect.

Alternative Budget Policies

The budget program we have suggested is by no means universally accepted. Many citizens object to planned deficits. Others have little faith in the ability of the President and his advisers, and ultimately of Congress, to select the proper magnitude and timing for tax rate changes, and still others feel that expenditure and tax changes are not potent weapons and will have little effect in any case. Many observers worry about the effect of a budget deficit on the public's attitude toward the "fiscal responsibility" of the government. This section will examine these objections briefly as well as some alternative budget proposals and their weaknesses.

The Annually Balanced Budget

From a Gallup poll taken in 1962,[2] public pronouncements by congressmen, and "letters to the editor," it is clear that a sizable segment of the public believes that the federal government should strive to balance the budget every year or at least that the federal government should not plan to run deficits. Those who hold this view usually draw an analogy to the family or private business budget. Since continuing deficits by individual families or businesses can mean economic ruin in the form of bankruptcy and loss of credit rating, they argue that deficits will have the same effect on the federal government. Some observers hold a more general view that the goal of an annually balanced budget is essential fiscal discipline to control the built-in tendency of the federal government to overspend.

There is something to be said for the concern for fiscal responsibility expressed by those who favor an annually balanced budget. If private spending is persistently weak and the government—in raising expenditures or lowering taxes to maintain full employment (or balance-of-payments equilibrium, as the case may be)—has to run

[2] See the *New York Times* of Aug. 2, 1962. Seventy-two percent of those polled were opposed to a tax cut if it meant that the federal government would go further into debt.

persistent deficits, the public may begin to feel that the extension of public services is essentially costless, and the result may be an over-extension of public services.[3] However, as a guide to fiscal action, the analogy between private bankruptcy and public bankruptcy is fallacious, as we will see in the next chapter.

An annually balanced budget could have extremely pernicious economic effects. Should the economy go into a slump, tax revenues would automatically decline and the budget would begin to show a deficit. If fiscal policy was directed toward the internal goal of offsetting this, the government would have to either decrease government spending or raise tax rates. In either case, the effect would be to lower the level of GNP still further, which would intensify the recession. Should the economy be rising, the attempt to maintain a balanced budget would work to accentuate any rise in GNP, accelerating the danger of inflation. In short, a serious attempt to maintain an annually balanced budget would reinforce any existing movement toward recession or inflation.

If fiscal policy were directed toward the external goal of payments equilibrium, a policy of annually balancing the budget would progressively increase a balance-of-payments surplus rather than eliminate it. Were the economy to enter a period of rapid growth in private demand, attempts to balance the budget would require expenditure increases and/or tax cuts, thus tending to increase a deficit in the balance of payments.

Whatever the merits of an annually balanced budget as a means of promoting fiscal responsibility, they are far outweighed by the perverse effects such a budget policy would be likely to have on the level of employment and prices. No responsible person could seriously advocate such a budget policy unless he could show that booms and slumps in business activity and the balance of payments are not significantly affected by fiscal actions and can be controlled effectively by other devices.

The Automatic Stabilizing Budget

While a policy of annually balanced budgets might accentuate the ups and downs of the economy and thus the problems of infla-

---

[3] On the other hand, if the federal government runs persistent surpluses, the public may feel that public services are really more costly than they are, and they may severely curtail spending.

tion and unemployment, a discretionary policy designed simply to promote full employment and stable prices also has inadequacies.

First, heavy reliance on the judgment of the executive branch and Congress to choose the proper level of tax rates and government spending poses problems because of the inadequacy of present forecasting techniques. A substantial amount of guesswork about future levels of output, prices, and employment is involved, and the possibility of error is ever present. Another difficulty with a discretionary policy is that it can easily lead to a primary emphasis on expenditure rather than tax changes, because the public's reaction against deficits caused by higher spending is known to be milder than that against deficits brought about by tax cuts. And finally, there is justifiable concern that a policy of "letting the deficits or surpluses occur where they may" removes the restraint on government spending provided by the goal of an annually balanced budget, in which every new expenditure has to be paid for by a clear and unequivocal act raising the necessary tax revenues.

There is a group of budget policy proposals designed to avoid the problems of either an annually balanced budget or a discretionary policy while preserving their virtues.

Perhaps the most widely known of these in this country is the "stabilizing budget" proposal of the Committee for Economic Development.[4] The proposal has had significant impact on the thinking of many influential citizens because it emanates from an organization of highly respected, top-echelon businessmen from all areas of industry and commerce. Briefly, the CED proposal suggests setting federal government purchases of goods and services at a "needs" level, fixing tax rates so that a "moderate surplus" would be generated at a "high employment" level of GNP,[5] and then letting the automatic fiscal stabilizers work to even out the periods of prosperity and recession in the economy.

The CED sees several virtues in the program. First, it would stabilize the economy; as was noted in our discussion of automatic

[4] See the committee's publications, *Taxes and the Budget: A Program for Prosperity in a Free Economy* (CED, 1947) and *Fiscal and Monetary Policy for High Employment* (CED, 1961).

[5] Both CED documents mentioned in footnote 4 define "high employment" as a situation where 96 percent of the labor force is employed. The "moderate surplus" is set at about $3 billion in the 1947 document and at something on the order of $3–7 billion in the 1961 document.

fiscal stabilizers in Chapter 5, fiscal stabilizers have been effective in the postwar period. Second, it would provide at least some of the budget discipline of the annually balanced budget; every new expenditure would require higher tax rates to maintain the planned surplus at high employment.[6] Finally, it would permit some retirement of the public debt, presuming that the economy would tend to fluctuate around the high employment level of GNP and that the surpluses in good years would be cumulatively greater than the deficits in bad years.

Very similar proposals have been made by Milton Friedman and Gunnar Myrdal.[7] The Friedman proposal differs from the CED proposal mainly in proposing that the budget be balanced at high employment and that federal deficits and surpluses be financed by issuing money or retiring money, respectively, rather than by issuing or retiring interest-bearing government securities. The Myrdal proposal, known as the "Swedish budget," differs mainly in that it provides for a cyclically balanced budget rather than a modest surplus over the cycle.

The automatic stabilizing budget programs are open to the same criticisms as the other types of budgets. First, although they do allow the automatic stabilizers to stabilize the economy, that is, to reduce the magnitude of the fluctuations in GNP, they do not necessarily stabilize it around the desired level—where there is full employment, price stability, and balance-of-payments equilibrium. Given government spending, as determined on a "needs" basis, and

---

[6] In terms of the graph used earlier to show the effects of several fiscal programs (p. 94), the CED proposal amounts to, first, selecting a budget line such as *A* or *B*. Then if government spending increases, taxes must also increase in order to keep the budget line in the same place and thus leave the surplus at high employment unchanged.

Actually, the CED proposal allows for changes in government spending unmatched by tax rate changes (1) where the surplus at high employment (96 percent) is growing because GNP is growing as the result of increases in the labor force and its productivity, (2) where there is an urgent need for an extraordinary expenditure of a temporary nature, and (3) in the event of a severe economic depression or major inflation.

[7] Friedman, "A Monetary and Fiscal Framework for Economic Stability," *American Economic Review*, June 1948, pp. 245–64, reprinted in his *Essays in Positive Economics* (University of Chicago Press, 1953), pp. 133–56; and Myrdal, "Fiscal Policy in the Business Cycle," *Amercan Economic Review*, March 1939, Supplement, pp. 183–93, reprinted in *Readings in Fiscal Policy*, edited by Arthur Smithies and J. Keith Butters (Richard D. Irwin, Inc., 1955), pp. 67–79.

the appropriate monetary policy, only one level of tax rates in a particular period of time will generate full employment and balance-of-payments equilibrium, and this level of tax rates (together with the planned amount of government expenditures) may result in either a surplus, a balanced budget, or a deficit at high (or full) employment. The goal of a moderate surplus or a balanced budget at full employment is not necessarily consistent with achieving the nation's internal and external goals at all times. Where full employment and external balance of payments can be achieved only with a planned deficit, a surplus or a balanced budget will only frustrate the objective. Where full employment, stable prices, and external balance are consistent only with a budget surplus, setting tax rates to produce a balanced budget, or too small a surplus, will tend to raise prices and produce a balance-of-payments deficit. In short, there can be no rigidly fixed rule as to the proper surplus or deficit at full employment GNP when the economy has more than one goal and one type of fiscal policy.

A second difficulty with this type of budget program arises from changes in the world situation or domestic crises that may call for substantial and frequent changes in government purchases of goods and services. Such events as the Korean war, the launching of Sputnik, the Berlin and Cuban crises, or the Vietnam conflict, which cannot be predicted, may cause sharp changes in federal spending. Under the stabilizing budget proposals, each unexpected change would call for corresponding changes in tax rates to maintain the planned surplus at high employment.[8] Aside from the impracticability of trying to secure such tax changes from Congress every time a change in expenditures is required, the initial effect of increases in government spending and taxes at full employment GNP would not be neutral. Even without emergency changes, there would be a slow and probably continuous rise in government expenditures due to normal population growth and the resulting demands for government services. If tax rates were raised correspondingly, the initial effect again would not be neutral.[9] As government expenditures rose,

[8] Although the CED budget proposal allows for extraordinary changes in federal spending without tax rate changes, it specifies that these should be temporary changes and in addition implies that they should not occur often. But they will occur often and in many cases will not be temporary.

[9] The *long-run* effects might be neutral if the effects of budget surpluses or deficits on private spending are considered (see footnote 11 in Chapter 5). How-

the budget surplus at full employment GNP would have to increase correspondingly to keep the same fiscal impact. So the "rule" prescribing a response to the budget surplus at full employment GNP would in any case have to be continuously revised, which makes the automatic budget considerably less automatic and much more discretionary.

These criticisms should not obscure the basic virtues of the automatic stabilizing budget proposals. They are unquestionably superior to the annually balanced budget as a guide to policy in that they recognize and accept the stabilizing effects of incurring deficits and/or surpluses as the automatic fiscal stabilizers operate over the course of a business cycle. Except for periods of chronically weak or excessive private demand and sharp changes in government spending, such a policy would probably produce reasonably good results. The chief danger is that a rule of fiscal policy such as that calling for "a moderate surplus at high employment" may become too rigidly established in the minds of policy makers and be adhered to even when it is clearly inappropriate.

Formula Flexibility

Another suggestion for an automatic budget policy is the "formula flexibility" proposal, whereby tax rate changes (and perhaps government expenditure changes) are legislated in advance, so that they will occur automatically with changes in certain indexes of business activity. For example, legislation might provide for an automatic tax cut if real GNP falls by a certain percentage or an automatic tax increase when there is a certain percentage rise in GNP. Provisions like these would produce the same effects as the automatic fiscal stabilizers.

This scheme has much that is appealing. It would avoid congressional delay in using tax rate changes as a stabilizing device and would add considerable potency to the fiscal arsenal. There would be very serious difficulties in implementation, however. First, price indexes and GNP data may at times give the wrong guidance, since they may reflect such temporary factors as strikes and crop failures rather than basic underlying trends. Second, even if the required for-

---

ever, an analysis of first-order effects, as we have seen in the previous chapter, shows that balanced changes in taxes and expenditures do affect planned spending.

mulas could be worked out, it is unlikely that Congress would be willing to delegate its control over taxes to this extent.

Summary and Conclusions

Expenditures and receipts of the federal government, by virtue of their magnitude, have considerable impact on the economy. If they were to be programmed without an awareness of their overall impact, the effects could be disastrous: extensive unemployment, serious inflationary pressures, or balance-of-payments disequilibrium.

A workable fiscal program has been suggested in this chapter that would include fixing the level of government purchases of goods and services on the basis of need, setting tax rates (given the proper monetary policy) so as to produce full employment GNP and balance-of-payments equilibrium regardless of the resulting budget deficit or surplus, and allowing the automatic fiscal stabilizers to reduce the size of periodic swings of GNP around the full employment level.

In examining several other types of fiscal program, we have seen that the concept of the annually balanced budget could produce serious economic instability if put into practice. Proposals for an automatic stabilizing budget—for fixing a goal of a certain budget surplus or deficit at full employment output and letting the automatic stabilizers work—have the merit of fiscal discipline but unfortunately impose rigid rules that are not necessarily the best response for many economic situations. Proposals for formula flexibility have much to recommend them but are probably too difficult to implement.

This discussion has assumed a lack of concern on the part of the public over the possibility of continued deficits in time of slack private demand. But the public apparently *is* considerably alarmed when planned deficits are incurred and the national debt increases. This leads us to the question of the national debt and its relation to fiscal policy, which will be discussed in the next chapter.

CHAPTER VII

Fiscal Policy and the National Debt

As was noted in Chapter 6, the federal government may have to run sizable deficits in times of weak private demand in order to raise planned spending to a high enough level to achieve full employment and balance-of-payments equilibrium. This means that there may be prolonged periods of increasing national debt, with no assurance that better times will produce the surpluses required to offset the deficits.

It is precisely this possibility that disturbs many critics of discretionary fiscal policy. In their view, increases in the national debt impose a burden on "future generations," aggravate inflationary tendencies, and threaten the nation's solvency. Their concern is voiced in statements such as the following by Senator John L. McClellan of Arkansas:

One of the greatest crimes of all . . . is one that is rarely considered by many Americans to be an offense at all. . . .

The full effects of this crime will not likely fall upon the generation that is committing it, but may call for reckoning far in the future, and, unless the present trend is reversed, each succeeding generation will pay more heavily for it. The offense is being compounded annually, and its long-range effects are cause for serious alarm. This is the crime: the generation that controls the economy of this nation today and those who have important government responsibility are callously and mercilessly burdening the livelihood and earnings of the generation that will follow us with a tremendous oppressive national debt. . . .

We are saddling our grandchildren . . . with the bills for our luxurious living. We have no moral right to do this. . . .[1]

In contrast, consider this statement of the Council of Economic Advisers in connection with the 1963 tax cut proposal:

. . . Under the present circumstances there is no reason to fear such increases in the public debt as tax reduction may entail. The ratio of interest payments on the debt to national income is small and is likely to fall, not rise. Nor is there any danger that the increase in the federal debt will be a burden on future generations. Tax reduction will increase investment, and hence the wealth we will bequeath, not decrease it. The danger is the opposite one. By failing to take expansionary fiscal action, we will keep both consumption and investment depressed, thus hurting not only ourselves, but future generations as well.[2]

Concern over the size and growth of the national debt is frequently reflected in actual or proposed congressional legislation. In 1961 Texas Congressmen James C. Wright and Frank Ikard, Jr., introduced a bill that would require that no less than 1 percent of the present debt be paid off annually until the entire debt was retired. Congress has long imposed a ceiling on the national debt and has shown considerable reluctance at times to raise it (although it has not hesitated to legislate the spending authority that makes the debt increase necessary).

Who is right? Is there or is there not a burden imposed by a national debt? Does the national debt lead to inflation and government bankruptcy? These questions are obviously crucial to the design of a fiscal program.

To simplify our discussion of the issue, we will assume that all federal debt is held by residents of the United States. This is not far from the actual situation, since currently more than 95 percent of federal debt is held domestically.

First, a definition of "national debt" is called for, a more controversial exercise than one might think. Next will follow a brief sum-

---

[1] "The Crime of National Insolvency," *Tax Review*, January 1964, pp. 2–3.
[2] *Economic Report of the President* (1963), p. 83.

mary of data relating the growth of the national debt to other economic magnitudes. The remainder of the chapter will deal with the issues surrounding the national debt: (1) the burden of the debt in a deficit setting that has resulted from attempts to alleviate unemployment by use of increased expenditures or reduced taxes; (2) the burden of the debt in a full employment setting; and (3) miscellaneous issues connected with the debt, such as inflation and national solvency.

Definition of the National Debt

The federal debt consists of direct obligations or debts of the U.S. Treasury and obligations of federal government enterprises or agencies. It is shown, as of June 30, 1967, in Table 11, broken down into "public debt"—that part issued by the Treasury—and "agency debt"—that part issued by federal agencies. The public debt consists of issues (that is, bonds, notes, and bills), which are generally sold to the public (some are held by federal agencies and trust funds), and "special issues," which are held only by government agencies and trust funds. Of the issues sold to the public, some are "marketable," that is, they are traded on securities markets, and some are

Table 11. Federal Debt, June 30, 1967

(In billions of dollars)

Item		Amount
Public debt (issued by Treasury)		322.9
Bills, certificates, and notes (marketable)	113.2	
Treasury bonds (marketable)	97.4	
U.S. savings bonds (nonmarketable)	51.2	
Other bonds (nonmarketable)[a]	1.5	
Special issues[b]	56.2	
Other	3.1	
Agency debt (issued by agencies)		18.5
Total gross federal debt[c]		341.3

Sources: *Federal Reserve Bulletin*, Vol. 54 (January 1968), p. A-36, and U.S. Bureau of the Budget, *The Budget of the United States Government, Fiscal Year 1969* (1968), p. 61. Details may not add to totals because of rounding.
  [a] Depository bonds, retirement plan bonds, foreign currency series, foreign series, and Rural Electrification Administration bonds.
  [b] Issued to U.S. government investment accounts.
  [c] Total includes noninterest-bearing debt, fully guaranteed securities, postal savings bonds, prewar bonds, adjusted service bonds, depository bonds, and armed forces leave bonds.

"nonmarketable" and cannot be traded (for example, U.S. savings bonds). The latter may, however, be redeemed in cash or converted into another issue.

As is shown in Table 11, what is usually referred to as the "national debt," or "public debt," was $322.9 billion in 1967. However, some writers, following Maurice Stans, would give a much larger figure—some $1 trillion—as the "true" national debt of the government of the United States.[3] Stans obtained the $1 trillion total by adding $700–800 billion to the national debt as usually estimated to cover what he considered to be reasonably firm commitments of the federal government to *future* expenditures under existing federal plans, broken down as follows (rounded figures in billions of dollars):

Past services		
Civil Service retirement	$	30
Military retirement		40
Veterans' program		300
Future services		
Unspent balances of prior year authorizations		40
Public assistance		50
Interstate highway system		30
Other (housing, public works, and so on)		30
Social security benefits		250–300
Total		$770–820

There are several misconceptions and errors in this tabulation. The most basic is considering planned future expenditures as a debt without matching them against planned future taxes. The result might indeed be a planned future increase in the debt, but it could just as well be a planned reduction. Even if it were assumed that Congress would not raise the necessary revenue to cover all of the government's spending commitments, only the uncovered amount would truly represent additional planned indebtedness. In any case, future congressional action on taxes or on spending commitments is impossible to predict, and any planned debt increase implied by such projections is at best a guess. This is not to say that awareness of such commitments for future spending is not important. It will

[3] Maurice Stans, director of the Bureau of the Budget under President Eisenhower, in a syndicated column headed "Uncle Sam Faces $1 Trillion Debt," in the *Washington Post*, Feb. 19, 1962. This column has been widely quoted in newspaper editorials and columns.

have implications for tax rate changes if for nothing else. But it is misleading to call all future expenditures under existing programs a "debt" of the federal government.

Furthermore, the compilation contains other errors. In the case of the social security trust funds, no account is taken of future tax increases written into the current law, which would substantially reduce the debt figure. The highway expenditures figure also makes no allowance for receipts from the special taxes earmarked for the highway trust fund. Mr. Stans uses different concepts for different items; for example, the figure for veterans' benefits is an estimate of total future expenditures under existing laws, while the figure for the retirement systems represents net future liability discounted to present value.

The principal causes of the growth of our federal debt have been wars and depressions. During World War I the federal debt rose sharply by about $22 billion to a level of $25.5 billion in 1919. From there it decreased some $9 billion to $16.2 billion in 1930. The economic depression of the thirties led to government deficit spending, and the federal debt increased by approximately $27 billion between June 1930 and June 1940. During World War II it grew tremendously, reaching $269.4 billion in June 1946. Since 1946 the debt has continued to grow, especially during years of recession, and it stood at $341.3 billion in June 1967.

A substantial amount of this debt is held by the Federal Reserve System ($46.7 billion) and by government investment accounts ($72.2 billion). For purposes of economic analysis, the net federal debt held by the public—gross federal debt minus the holdings of the Federal Reserve System and government accounts—rather than the gross debt is the relevant figure. The net public debt stood at $222.4 billion in June 1967.[4]

The fact that most of the growth of the debt occurred during major wars does not in itself mean that debt inevitably accompanies war. In World War II, in particular, taxes were set too low relative to expenditures to prevent serious price pressures from developing. Rather than raise taxes sufficiently to reduce planned spending to a

[4] For more discussion and detail on the growth of the public debt, see Marshall A. Robinson, *The National Debt Ceiling: An Experiment in Fiscal Policy* (Brookings Institution, 1959), pp. 20–25.

level consistent with stable prices, the government used price controls and rationing to suppress inflation. The rationale for this was that to raise taxes sufficiently to finance the war without inflation would have seriously impaired work incentives. Whether this rationale was in fact correct is now difficult to assess. If correct, it points to a serious limitation on the use of fiscal policy in periods of large defense outlays. There is evidence, however, that income taxes do not have a very important effect on work incentives.[5] Furthermore, it is hard to see why the same patriotic fervor used to sell savings bonds could not have been channeled into exhortations to work, if indeed work incentives were affected.

Data on the Federal Debt

Merely looking at the growth of the net federal debt in isolation reveals little except that it has grown tremendously over the years the U.S. government has been in existence, from $75 million in 1791 to about $222.4 billion as of June 1967 (or about 3,000 times over). But so have other economic measures, in particular the volume of output and private debt. Likewise, federal net interest payments have grown immensely over the years, but so has our ability to carry them.

To get some perspective on the growth of the national debt, it is useful to make the comparisons shown in Figures 14–16. Figure 14 shows, for five-year intervals from 1900 to 1930 and annually thereafter, the net federal debt and the ratio of the net federal debt to GNP (in current dollars). The debt-GNP ratio was very low up to 1916, rose sharply during World War I, and then declined through the 1920's. In the 1930's it began another rise, which continued through World War II. It has fallen since and is currently back almost to the levels that prevailed in the middle and late 1930's. In Figure 15 the growth of federal debt is compared with the growth of nonfederal debt since 1900. The figure shows clearly that federal

[5] See J. Keith Butters, Lawrence E. Thompson, and Lynn L. Bollinger, *The Effect of Taxation on Investments by Individuals* (Harvard University, Graduate School of Business Administration, 1953); George F. Break, "Income Taxes and Incentives To Work: An Empirical Study," *American Economic Review,* Vol. 47 (September 1957), pp. 529–49; and James N. Morgan, Robin Barlow, and Harvey E. Brazer, *Economic Behavior of the Affluent* (Brookings Institution, 1966).

FIGURE 14. Net Federal Debt at Five-Year Intervals, 1900–30, and Annually, 1931–67[a]

Billions of dollars

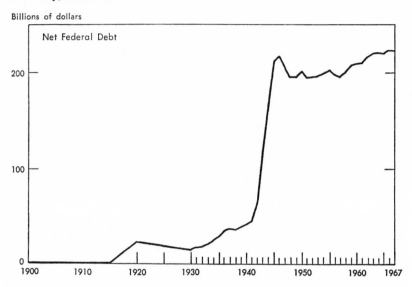

Sources: Raymond W. Goldsmith, A Study of Saving in the United States (Princeton University Press, 1955), Vol. 1, p. 985; Board of Governors of the Federal Reserve System, Banking and Monetary Statistics (FRS, 1943), pp. 509, 510, 512, and Federal Reserve Bulletin, Vol. 36 (December 1950), p. 1658; Executive Office of the President/U.S. Bureau of the Budget, The Budget in Brief, 1969 (1968), p. 71; and U.S. Treasury Department, Treasury Bulletin, December 1967, p. 68.

Percent of GNP

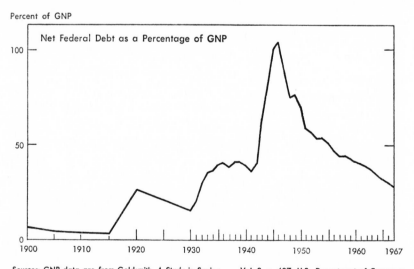

Sources: GNP data are from Goldsmith, A Study in Saving . . . , Vol. 3, p. 427; U.S. Department of Commerce The National Income and Product Accounts . . . , pp. 2–3; and Economic Report of the President (1968), p. 209.
[a] Net debt figures for 1900–50 include Treasury securities outstanding and Treasury-guaranteed issues of government agencies. Data for 1951–67 include nonguaranteed agency debt and exclude Treasury debt issued to international lending organizations. Thus the data for 1951–67 are consistent with the new, unified budget, but the series has not been extended back to cover the earlier period.

FIGURE 15. Federal and Nonfederal Debt, 1920–66

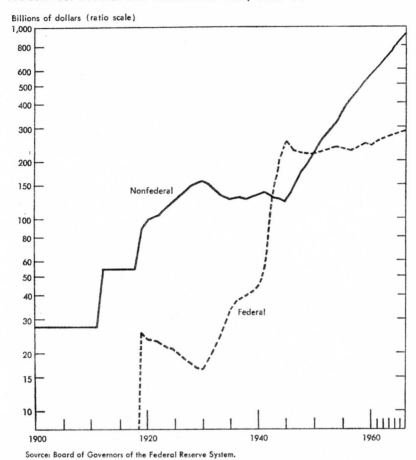

Source: Board of Governors of the Federal Reserve System.

debt grew faster than nonfederal debt during the periods 1917–19 and 1930–45 but that in the other 48 years of the 67-year period nonfederal debt grew faster.[6]

Finally, Figure 16 shows net interest paid on the federal debt, both in dollars and as a percentage of GNP. Since 1900, interest paid on the federal debt has not exceeded 2.0 percent of GNP—a level reached just after World War II. The percentage fell to 1.4 in 1951 and was 1.2 percent in 1955. The growth of federal debt, then, though large in absolute terms, appears less awesome when related to the growth of output or of private debt.

[6] Because the vertical axes in Figure 15 are a ratio scale, the slopes, or "steepness," of the lines show the rates of growth of public and private debt.

FIGURE 16. Net Gross Interest Paid on Federal Debt at Five-Year Intervals, 1900–30, and Annually, 1931–66

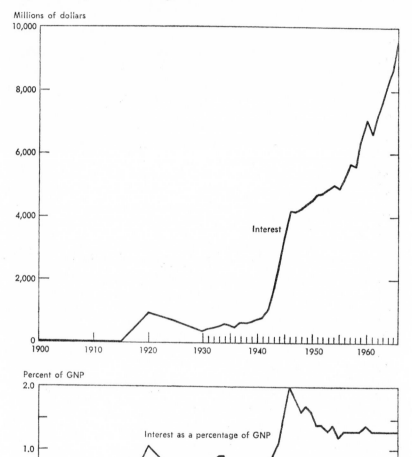

Sources: Data for 1900–25 are from Goldsmith, A *Study of Saving* . . . , Vol. 3, p. 445; and for 1930–66, from U.S. Department of Commerce.

The Burden of the Debt in an Unemployment Setting

As was noted at the outset, hostility to the size of the national debt as well as to its continued growth generally arises from the view that the debt will impose a burden on future generations. To decide whether this view is justified, we will first consider a society where there is unemployment and where the government plans to run a deficit to finance additional expenditures or to cut taxes in order to restore output to a full employment level. The issue then is, Does government borrowing to finance a planned deficit create a burden for future generations?

In one sense at least, there is clearly no burden on later generations. *A closed society cannot dispose of more goods and services than it currently produces; it cannot borrow tomorrow's output today.* In a period of unemployment there is essentially no competition between the government and the private sector for resources. Goods and services acquired by the government at the time of the expenditure do not reduce the output available to consumers or private investors. In fact, as we have seen in Chapter 5, increases in government spending or cuts in taxes tend to have a "multiplier effect," that is, tend to stimulate increases both in private spending and consumption. In short, deficit financing to restore full employment leaves future generations better off to the extent that private investment is stimulated, for, in the absence of an expenditure increase or tax cut, the added investment would probably not take place and future generations would have a smaller stock of private capital and lower output. A further gain in future output results from government spending of an investment type, for example, for schools, bridges, and roads.

What about the interest payments on the debt and possibly the repayment of the principal that fall to the lot of future generations? Are these not a burden? The answer is no. There is no aggregate burden on future generations who have to make interest payments on the debt and perhaps repay the principal, for these are simply *transfers* of income (or wealth) among members of society. There may indeed be "distributional effects"—wealth may be redistributed from taypayers to bondholders to the extent that these are not the same individuals—but these do not necessarily leave the community in worse circumstances in the aggregate. In summary, deficit financing and increases in the national debt do not impose a burden on future generations in an unemployment setting. In fact, running deficits to promote full employment leaves future generations better off in terms of increased real output and investment. In this setting at least, intergeneration equity is not violated.[7]

The Burden of the Debt in a Full Employment Setting

Now consider a society that is always at full employment regardless of what the government does or does not do about spending, taxes, and the like. Assume that the government plans to spend an

---

[7] Franco Modigliani has come to a somewhat different conclusion on this question. He reasons that under certain conditions a deficit created to boost the economy from a depression or recession can leave future generations in worse circumstances than if no government action had been taken. Suppose recessions or depressions are temporary, that is, that the economy will recover eventually even if no government action is taken. Suppose further that consumers and firms together have a plan of desired capital accumulation. A recession, then, will reduce the present generation's capital below the desired level, since saving and investment are reduced as income falls. The reduction in capital below the desired level will force the members of the present generation to cut their consumption over their lifetimes (even after full employment is restored) to an extent equal to the loss in capital accumulation during the period of unemployment. In short, they will have to save more to accumulate the capital "lost" during the recession. The higher rate of capital formation after full employment is restored will tend to build the stock of capital back to the level that could have been expected if there had been no temporary unemployment by the time the recession generation disappears. On the other hand, if the government acts to combat the recession and creates new debt in doing so, the new debt to some extent will replace the "lost" capital in the net worth of investors. Thus the present generation will not seek to build the capital stock back to the planned level; it will be content with government bonds rather than physical capital. Later generations may thus have less private capital than if the government had not attacked the recession by running a deficit.

Of course, the crux of Modigliani's argument is his assumption that recessions are in fact temporary and that government debt is unproductive. If, however, budget deficits are financed by issuing money, and if asset holders receive a stream of real returns from holding money or if money is a "factor of production," then even in Modigliani's argument, debt financing need not impose a burden, whether it occurs in a full employment or unemployment setting. See his article "Long-Run Implications of Alternative Fiscal Policies and the Burden of the National Debt," *Economic Journal,* December 1961, p. 731. For additional discussion of the burden of the debt from the point of view stressing the supply of capital, see Peter A. Diamond, "National Debt in a Neoclassical Growth Model," *American Economic Review,* December 1965, esp. p. 1141.

additional $100. Will it make any difference, in terms of a burden on future generations, if that expenditure is debt-financed or tax-financed?

Because of full employment, goods and services acquired by the government must always be paid for by a reduction in the output available to the private sector at the time of the expenditure. So, whether tax-financed or debt-financed, the expenditure is immediate; it cannot possibly be paid for by future generations, and thus there is no burden on them in this sense.

As far as interest payments on the debt and possibly repayment of the principal are concerned, here, too, as in the unemployment setting, no burden in the aggregate is imposed on future generations. These are simply transfers of income (or wealth) among members of society.

However, while it is true that a closed community cannot increase today's output by borrowing tomorrow's, the way in which today's output is used can affect the output of tomorrow, and debt-financing has a different impact on the use of today's output from tax-financing. It is through this impact that debt-financing of expenditures may impose a burden on future generations.

If the economy is at full employment, then, by definition, the increase in government spending cannot increase total output. Prices will rise whether the increase in government spending is debt-financed or tax-financed.[8] But how is investment affected? Suppose an increase in government spending of $100 is debt-financed. Taxes on private income, and therefore private disposable (after tax) income, will be unchanged. If we assume that private consumption depends only on the level of disposable personal income of consumers and that private investment depends only on interest rates (credit conditions), then private consumption of goods will remain unchanged. Because private consumption outlays will be unaffected (and government expenditures will be increasing), a decrease in the private use of output must come and (according to our assumptions) it will fall on private investment. Debt-financing of an expenditure, then, will tend to result in a fall in private investment by the amount of the increase in government spending.[9]

---

[8] As noted in Chapter 5, an increase in government spending has a larger multiplier effect than an equal increase in taxes, and thus when taxes are raised to finance government spending, the net effect is expansionary and prices will rise.

[9] Under different assumptions, debt-financing need not lead to a fall in private

How does this result compare with the result of tax-financing a like amount? In the latter case, some part of the tax increase will come out of private personal income. Private consumption will decline by some fraction of this reduction in disposable personal income, but not all since, as was noted earlier, consumers in the aggregate do not reduce consumption by the total amount of a decrease in disposable personal income. The balance of the impact will fall then on private investment. This means that both private consumption and investment will fall, with the total decline in both being just equal to the total increase in government spending.

A comparison of the two cases reveals that, although investment falls in both the debt-financed and tax-financed cases, it falls farther in the former. Here lies the burden on future generations. The burden can be measured in terms of the loss of potential output that will result from the loss of potential private capital. That is, debt-financing will reduce private investment more than tax-financing the same amount, thereby leaving future generations with less capital equipment for production and thus restricting them to a lower level of private output. Although both debt-financing and tax-financing leave future generations with less private capital and thus less output, debt-financing leaves them relatively worse off.[10]

Nothing has been said thus far about the effect of the use of government expenditures, and government outlays have implicitly been assumed to be unproductive. But government expenditures are not unproductive. They may be less, or more, productive than private investment. If government expenditures are less productive than, or equally as productive as, private investment, our conclusions about the relative burden still hold. If, however, government expenditures are more productive, future generations will be better off with the expenditures than without them, whether debt-financed or tax-financed. But they will be relatively less well off with debt-financing than with tax-financing. There will still be a greater burden in a full employment setting imposed by debt-financing than by tax-financing, in the sense that the gain to future generations will be smaller.[11]

investment by an amount equal to the increase in government spending. To some extent it may reduce consumer credit rather than investment credit.

[10] Note again that if money is "productive," and if the debt-financing consists of money issues, then even here there may be no burden from debt-financing.

[11] Some economists, notably E. J. Mishan, dispute the validity of the argument

In summary, deficit financing and increases in the national debt in a full employment setting do not necessarily impose an absolute burden on future generations. If government expenditures are more productive than private investment, future generations will be better off with debt-financed expenditures than without such expenditures. However, it is also clear that, in this setting, future generations will benefit relatively more from such expenditures if they are financed by increasing taxes rather than by increasing the federal debt.

Deficits and Other Issues

Some newspaper and magazine writers and pamphleteers make categorical statements to the effect that "the increasing debt (deficit) is inflationary," linking together hostility to deficits and an increasing national debt and the general desire to avoid inflation. But as we have already noted in Chapter 6, the deficit (or "full employment deficit") is not a reliable measure of fiscal policy. A large deficit can result from a severe anti-inflationary fiscal policy if the government tightens up too much and induces a recession—or if expenditures drop in the private sector and the economy goes into a recession—and federal tax receipts fall as GNP declines. Large deficits occurred in the 1940's during a period of high employment and upward price pressure (which was suppressed by price and wage controls). During an earlier period, 1931–34, however, large deficits occurred during a period of severe unemployment and falling prices. Thus there is no basis for using the actual deficit or surplus to measure the inflationary or deflationary impact of federal fiscal action.

---

that a greater burden is imposed on future generations by borrowing than by taxing, even in a full employment setting. Mishan argues that since taxes reduce present consumption and borrowing reduces private capital for future generations, if one talks about a burden being imposed on future generations by borrowing, there is an equal obligation to consider the burden imposed on the present generation by taxing. Every decision society undertakes today affects future generations. Thus decisions to debt-finance government expenditures are no more of a burden on future generations than are decisions by individuals to consume rather than to invest. "After all, we could enormously increase provision for the future if we performed heroic feats of austerity during our lifetimes. Are we then not imposing a heavy burden on these future generations to the extent that we eschew these heroic feats of austerity and instead follow the path of our wonted self-indulgence?" ("How To Make a Burden of the Public Debt," *Journal of Political Economy*, December 1963, p. 540).

It is often implied that all inflation is due to increasing federal outlays, or that private and state-local outlays are not inflationary but that federal government outlays are. It is said, too, that private or state and local government outlays are productive whereas federal government outlays are unproductive. GNP is said to be an inaccurate measure of a nation's output, primarily because it includes in total output these unproductive government purchases of goods and services.

Such arguments show a faulty understanding of what determines a nation's output, the nature of output, and the causes of inflation or depression. If government purchases of goods and services are unproductive, society might just as well discontinue such outlays and use the resources thus freed in the private sector. It could eliminate expenditures on missiles, planes, courts, police, highways, and education and use the resources to produce more cars, electric shavers, houses, and private planes. It should be obvious that federal (as well as state and local) government expenditures *are* productive in the sense that they satisfy certain social needs that are not met by the private market. These social needs are determined by elected representatives, who are responsible to the electorate.

It should be clear also that increases in private outlays for consumption and investment can at times be responsible for inflationary pressures, as they were in the period 1946–48. Whether private or government spending is at the root of inflation, the important thing is to bring about a reduction in aggregate spending.

The Public Debt and National Bankruptcy

There is a great deal of emotion in people's attitudes toward the public debt. For example, statements are frequently made to the effect that, if the national debt reaches some particular level, the government's credit standing will be impaired and disaster will follow in the form of something casually referred to as "national bankruptcy." While it is difficult to evaluate these statements, the idea is not a new one that there is a definite limit to the size of the national debt that can be carried without disaster. Individuals have long predicted that a debt of one-tenth, one-fifth, or one-half of the amount we now have would result in national bankruptcy, and they have had to revise the limit upward when it was indeed passed and ruin failed to follow.

How much can the federal government borrow? Is there a point beyond which borrowing would have to cease because people would refuse to lend? To answer these questions, one must understand the basis for the credit standing of governments, whether federal, state, or local. Governments have a power not shared by other borrowers —they can impose taxes with which to pay interest on their debt and repay the principal. As long as a government does not abuse its taxing power, it will have the ability to borrow. It may have to pay higher interest charges if its debt becomes quite large, but it can borrow as long as it is willing to do so. And this is not all; central governments also have the power to coin and print money. They can always do this, instead of imposing taxes, to meet interest costs on their debts, and as long as they choose to do so, they can continue to borrow.

As a matter of fact, the securities of the U.S. Treasury are looked on by investors as a nearly riskless investment (from the standpoint of defaulting on interest payments), despite the enormous increase in the debt in the last half-century.

This does not mean that we should not worry about deficits and the growth of the debt. If the debt is growing because private demand is weak and the government is pursuing a policy of stimulating the economy with tax reduction (or expenditure increases), the deficit is not only harmless but a benefit to the health of the economy. If private spending is strong, however, and prices are rising, then low tax rates and a deficit are poor policy indeed. In short, there are good deficits and bad deficits. Good deficits occur when fiscal policy is used to stimulate the economy or to cushion it against economic declines. Bad deficits occur when, in the face of strong private spending, government refuses to raise taxes (given a planned level of government expenditures) to eliminate inflationary pressures.

The Psychological Effects

It has been held that, even though there may be no danger of burdening future generations, the stimulative effects of increasing the public debt to counteract recessions may be negated or partially offset by public hostility to debt increases. That is, irrational, unwarranted fear of such increases may reduce private spending (particularly investment), which will offset the stimulative effect of the fiscal action producing the deficit. Businessmen may say, "With such fiscal irresponsibility in the White House, I will not commit my company to new capital outlays."

On the other hand, the announcement itself of stimulative federal fiscal actions may have quite the opposite effect. The stock market's reaction to tax cut suggestions in 1963 and comments in the business press suggest that such positive fiscal action actually encourages business optimism and stimulates investment.

There is no clear answer as to which effect is likely to be dominant. It is hard to single out the effect on businessmen's expectations of a single action of an administration, such as incurring a planned deficit. It is probably true that the overall image of an administration has an important psychological influence on business investment decisions. It is not clear what influence a deficit by itself has or how strong that influence may be.

Summary and Conclusions

From the discussion in this chapter, it is clear that deficits may be economically defensible and even desirable under a great many conditions. They are unjustified, of course, when the economy is at full employment and there are inflationary pressures. If deficits are incurred as part of a rounded program to restore full employment, however, they are all to the good. They tend to increase output and employment and impose no easily identifiable real burden on future generations. Future interest payments and the repayment of principal are essentially financial transfers involving no aggregate real burden. Arguments to the effect that increasing the federal debt will somehow lead to national ruin or bankruptcy have little foundation in fact. And while there may be adverse psychological effects from deficits, there may just as well be salutary ones.

CHAPTER VIII

Determining the Level of Federal Spending

THE AMOUNT OF FEDERAL spending and taxes needed to stabilize the economy has been shown to depend, at least in part, on the state of the economy. When private demand for goods and services is strong, stabilization may call for restraint in expenditures on goods and services, higher tax rates (or a reduction in transfer payments), or both. When private demand is weak, federal taxes may need to be adjusted downward (or transfer payments upward), expenditures to be increased, or both.

Clearly, however, there are other grounds for judging the level of federal spending besides its total effect on employment, prices, growth, and the balance of payments. Expenditures on nuclear submarines, defense personnel, or defense research, for example, cannot readily be adjusted up or down as private demand weakens or becomes buoyant. Nor can old age pensions and retirement benefits under social security be juggled to offset ups or downs in private spending, although the timing of payments can be accelerated when necessary. Interest payments on the federal debt, highway construction, and public health are other examples of federal programs that are difficult to vary for countercyclical reasons. While the total amount of spending may be evaluated with an eye to the current

125

state of the economy and while this evaluation may in turn affect budget decisions on particular programs, the basis for judging individual federal spending programs cannot be solely, or even primarily, their impact on the level of economic activity.

As was stated in Chapter 6, setting the level of federal purchases of goods and services involves choosing between private and public use of resources. Thus some criterion is needed to guide the policy maker in making such a choice. Decisions concerning the level of transfer payments (the transfer of resources between individuals) or grants-in-aid (the transfer of funds between the federal government and the states and their subdivisions) clearly require different criteria from those needed to determine the level of government expenditures on goods and services. What are these or what should they be?

What criteria can the citizen use, apart from those of stabilization, as a basis for determining whether the overall level of spending or the amounts to be spent on different programs are appropriate? Certainly, people have views on these matters, as editorial pages, letters to editors, and casual conversations clearly indicate. They may complain about "wild-eyed spenders," or deplore the neglect of certain federal programs, or both. Yet if they are pressed to explain their views about federal spending proposals in greater detail, they seldom seem to have objective criteria for judging the need for or proper level of federal spending. They may defend a particular program by saying it will "help the community," "create jobs," "meet human needs," or "keep (my) industry prosperous." Or they may attack programs as "unnecessary," "involving a concentration of power in Washington," "better left to the local community," or "profligate and wasteful."

This chapter will investigate other criteria for judging federal spending than stabilization policy and the extent to which they have been used in determining the level of federal spending.

Purposes of Federal Spending

The basic data for our investigation are presented in Table 12, where federal expenditures for 1966 are classified according to function and type (purchases of goods and services, transfer payments, grants-in-aid, and so on). Several general features of federal expen-

Table 12. Federal Expenditures by Function, 1966

(Dollars amounts in billions)

Item	Purchases of goods and services	Transfer payments and net interest paid	Grants-in-aid to state and local governments	Subsidies less current surplus of government enterprises	Total	Percentage of total[a]
(1)						
National defense	60.5	1.5	0.4	—0.1	62.3	43.6
Space research and technology	5.9	—	b	—	5.9	4.1
General government, except net interest paid	2.2	1.9	0.1	—0.1	4.1	2.9
International affairs and finance	0.6	2.3	b	b	2.9	2.0
Subtotal	69.2	5.7	0.5	—0.2	75.2	52.6
(2)						
Health and hospitals	1.0	0.4	0.8	—	2.2	1.5
Education	0.4	0.3	2.6	b	3.4	2.4
Transportation	1.4	b	4.2	0.2	5.8	4.1
Regulation of commerce and finance	0.1	—	—	—	0.1	0.1
Postal services	0.1	—	—	1.0	1.1	0.8
Civilian safety	0.1	—	—	—	0.1	0.1
Natural resources	2.3	b	0.3	—0.2	2.4	1.7
Subtotal	5.4	0.7	7.9	1.0	15.1	10.6
(3)						
Public assistance and relief	b	b	3.9	—	3.9	2.7
Old age and retirement benefits	0.5	22.1	—	—	22.4	15.7
Other social security and special welfare	0.5	0.6	1.2	b	2.3	1.6
Labor	0.3	0.2	0.5	—	1.0	0.7
Veterans' benefits and services	1.5	4.9	b	b	6.4	4.5
Agriculture and agricultural resources	—1.1	—	0.2	5.0	4.1	2.9
Unemployment benefits paid	—	1.8	—	—	1.8	1.3
Housing and community development	0.4	b	0.6	—0.3	0.7	0.5
Subtotal	2.1	29.6	6.4	4.7	42.6	29.8
(4)						
Net interest paid	b	9.5	—	—	9.5	6.6
Subtotal	b	9.5	—	—	9.5	6.6
Total expenditures[a]	77.0[c]	45.6	14.8	5.4	142.9[c]	100.0[c]

Source: *Survey of Current Business*, July 1967 ,p. 29.

[a] Details may not add to totals because of rounding.

[b] Less than 0.05.

[c] Includes expenditures of $0.3 billion for "Other commerce, transportation, and housing" not shown separately.

ditures should be noted. Out of a total of about $143 billion, only $77 billion represent purchases of goods and services. Transfer payments—involving not payment for services but old age benefits, retirement benefits, and the like—account for $36 billion, and interest paid on the debt amounts to over $9 billion. Another $15 billion represents grants-in-aid to state and local governments.

The functional breakdown of federal expenditures discloses some interesting facts. The importance of defense spending is obvious; it accounts for half of the total. Second in importance are old age and retirement benefit payments, which account for about one-seventh of the total. If net interest payments of $9.5 billion are added to national defense and space research expenditures and old age and retirement benefits, these items alone account for three-fourths of total spending—some $100 billion in 1966. All the other programs of the federal government—foreign aid, agriculture, natural resources, transportation, veterans' benefits, and public assistance—make up only one-fourth of total spending.

How can one decide what the federal government *should* do in each of these areas?

Federal versus State-Local Responsibility

First of all we must consider what types of programs come within the responsibility of the federal government as opposed to that of the states and their subdivisions. The legal division of responsibility among the various levels of government is found in the Constitution and in court interpretations of it. The Constitution divides the powers of government: those of the national government are specified (Art. I, Sec. 8), while those of the states and their subdivisions are residual. The Tenth Amendment reserves to the states all powers not granted to the national government or prohibited to the states. The federal government (through Congress) was given the power "to lay and collect taxes, duties, imposts, and excises, to pay the debts, and provide for the common defense and general welfare of the United States," which was intended to restrict severely the scope of federal activity.[1] There is no specific mention of spending for highways, public health, education, or public welfare, here or anywhere else in the Constitution; and since the Tenth Amendment does not deny these powers to the states, they are presumed to be residual powers of the states.

Until the 1930's the courts were very reluctant to allow the national government to assume powers beyond those necessary to provide for national defense and to regulate interstate trade and commerce, and the Congress was generally reluctant to seek more respon-

[1] James A. Maxwell, *Financing State and Local Governments* (rev. ed.; Brookings Institution, 1969), Chap. 1, esp. p. 12.

sibilities. As a result, in 1927 the federal government accounted for less than one-fifth of total government expenditures for civilian purposes—17 percent.[2]

However, during the decade of the 1930's, with the problems and pressures of the greatest economic depression in United States history, there developed a shift in social philosophy and judicial thinking. The judicial interpretation of the Constitution that emerged in the 1930's "accepted a reading of the general welfare clause that placed no discernible judicial limits on the amounts or purposes of federal spending. . . ."[3] During this period the federal share of civilian expenditures rose to 42 percent (1938), and it has remained above 35 percent since that time.[4] In short, the powers of the national government to tax and spend have come to be interpreted very broadly and now cover many areas of spending formerly reserved exclusively to the states and their subdivisions, for example, public welfare, relief, and public health. Thus there are generally no precise legal boundaries to the areas of responsibility of the various levels of government.[5]

The division of responsibility among levels of government with regard to spending and taxation is now a question mainly for legislative and executive judgment. Such a judgment generally employs at least two criteria. One of these is efficiency. Congress and the President nearly always consider whether or not a particular program can be carried out most efficiently at the federal level or at some other level. Some activities, such as sewage treatment and garbage disposal, can clearly be performed most efficiently at the local level. Others, such as policing of highway traffic, can be most efficiently performed by state governments. Still others, like national defense and postal service, can achieve the greatest economies when undertaken by the federal government. Aside from these areas, about which there is little dispute, there is a host of activities, such as education, medical care for the aged, public health, and highway construction, about which there may be pronounced differences of opinion as to the level that can most efficiently provide the service. In

---

[2] *Ibid.,* p. 16.

[3] Commission on Intergovernmental Relations, *A Report to the President* (1955), p. 29, quoted in *ibid.,* p. 20.

[4] Maxwell, *Financing State and Local Governments,* p. 16 (Chart 1–1 B).

[5] There are exceptions to this statement. For example, the provision of police protection is a responsibility still reserved to the states.

any case, virtually all proposals for federal as against state and local spending are judged in part on the basis of efficiency.

Another criterion is political ideology. Many fear undue expansion of federal activity, for example, because they believe individual freedom, liberty, and political participation are best preserved by keeping government activities at the lowest level possible, that is, by decentralization. In their view, keeping government activity at the lowest level possible makes for closer contact among the persons receiving the services, those paying the taxes, and the government officials who make policy and administer the programs. Transfer of these activities, or portions of them, to higher government levels may mean that decisions are no longer made by government officials familiar with the circumstances, needs, and desires of those affected.

The two criteria—efficiency and decentralization—often conflict. A particular program might be most efficiently administered at the federal level, but it might also create, in the minds of many persons, an undesirable, additional concentration of power at that level. In such cases, the public, through its elected representatives, must choose. There is no way to say which criterion—efficiency or decentralization—should be given more weight.

The issue of the proper level of government to carry out particular programs should be distinguished from the issue of the proper level of government to raise revenue. Society may decide, for example, that highway construction is best carried out at the state and local level but that it should be financed with federal funds. In the past three decades, a whole host of state and local programs have been partially or wholly federally financed through the grant-in-aid mechanism. These programs may be strictly regulated and controlled by the federal government through a set of standards and requirements imposed on the states and localities receiving the funds, or the amount of federal control may be minimal. The fact that the federal tax system is very efficient in raising revenues has led in recent years to a number of proposals to make block grants-in-aid to states, to refund a portion of federal revenues raised in each state to the state and its subdivisions, or to share federal tax revenues on some formula basis with state and local governments.[6]

[6] For details, see Joseph A. Pechman, "Financing State and Local Government," in American Bankers Association, *Proceedings of a Symposium on Federal Taxation* (The Association, 1965) (Brookings Reprint 103); Walter W. Heller, *New*

The criteria for determining the proper governmental level for financing programs have not been thoroughly investigated by economists. One important consideration, however, would seem to be the extent to which the benefits from state and local programs are national as well as local in nature, that is, the extent to which benefits "spill over" and benefit the nation as a whole as well as the states and localities. Beyond this, about all that can be said is that the two criteria we mentioned above for determining the proper level of government for particular programs also apply in some degree to the issue of the source of financing. Certainly, whether programs are financed by the federal government or the state and local governments will have considerable bearing on the degree of decentralization of governmental activities. The source of revenue may also affect the efficiency with which programs are carried out.

For the purposes of this chapter, however, let us suppose that the crucial issue of the division of responsibility between the federal government and the states for programs and financing is resolved. That is, let us suppose the federal government has certain clearly defined areas of responsibility. In this setting, then, how big should the federal budget be? How much should the federal government spend on national defense? Agriculture? Old-age assistance?

Spending on Public Goods

Consider the federal spending programs in group 1 in Table 12, that is, national defense, space research and technology, general government (except net interest), and international affairs. This group of federal expenditures amounted to $75.2 billion in 1966. Of this total, $69.2 billion was for purchases of goods and services, and $5.7 billion was for transfer payments. Grants-in-aid and subsidies (less the current surplus) of government enterprises were negligible.

As Table 12 shows, this group accounted for 53 percent of total federal expenditures in 1966. The goods and services included in this group are clearly of the kinds that, if they were not provided by government, would not be provided at all.

Dimensions of Political Economy (W. W. Norton, 1967), Chap. 3; and Walter W. Heller and Joseph A. Pechman, "Questions and Answers on Revenue Sharing," in *Revenue Sharing and Its Alternatives: What Future for Fiscal Federalism?* Hearings before the Subcommittee on Fiscal Policy of the Joint Economic Committee, 90 Cong. 1 sess. (1967), pp. 111–17 (Brookings Reprint 135).

These kinds of goods and services are usually referred to as "public goods." The most common characteristic of public goods is that they are available to all individuals independent of each individual's tax contributions. Probably the best example is national defense. Every citizen of the United States benefits to some degree from the security provided by the armed forces regardless of what share of the cost he may bear. Another characteristic of public goods and services is that their use by any one individual or group does not reduce the amount available for any other individual or group. This is not true of most private goods. Since the benefits resulting from public goods accrue to society as a whole, a market price for units of the goods or services cannot possibly be established. Who would provide nuclear submarines and army divisions if the federal government did not? Public goods are usually financed through general taxation.

In order to determine the level of federal spending on public goods, the following questions must clearly be separated. First, how much of society's resources should be devoted to the production of public goods for which the federal government is responsible? Second, how much should be spent on defense as compared with international affairs, the space program, and so on; that is, how should the total public goods budget be allocated among the various alternatives? Finally, given a specific budget for the production of a certain public good—for example, the defense budget—how should the total amount be allocated among alternative means of accomplishing the goal of national security?

The first of these questions is the most difficult to answer. Societies face scarcity—scarcity of resources as compared with wants. Thus the members of society have to assess the relative benefits of alternative uses. For example, if they decide to devote a portion of their resources to space exploration so that a man may reach the moon by a certain date, they must give up the use of that portion for other purposes, that is, they must be satisfied with fewer television sets, cars, boats, and the like. Since the provision of public goods requires that resources be diverted from private to public use, a criterion is needed for deciding on the proper level of spending on public goods. If some basis could be found for evaluating the benefits and costs to society of public goods, a comparison of these benefits and costs might provide such a criterion. Theoretically, then, benefit-cost comparisons could be used to determine the optimum level of spending on public goods.

Unfortunately, the task of estimating society's benefits and costs from each unit of federal expenditure on public goods is difficult.[7] As an example, let us consider defense expenditures again. How can we estimate the additional benefits to society from additional units of defense—such as one more nuclear submarine? The cost to society of providing an additional nuclear submarine is the additional quantity of private goods and services (refrigerators, television sets, and so on) that must be given up in order to provide the resources for the submarine. As important as certain private goods may be, there is no way to tell whether society's benefits from an additional nuclear submarine exceed or fall short of society's costs in giving up these private goods.

The second question—how much should be spent on alternative public goods—entails a comparison of the benefits and costs of one public good vis à vis those of another. Given the overall level of federal spending on public goods, the essential comparison here is between the benefits derived from the last dollar spent on one public good and that spent on another. Here we are applying a basic (and very old) economic criterion that dictates that expenditures on a good or service should be continued only to the point where the benefit derived from the last dollar spent is equalized. As far as spending on public goods is concerned, when the benefits from the last dollar spent on one public good (for example, defense) fall short of those derived from another public good (for example, international affairs), then funds should be reallocated to the latter good to achieve a higher total gain for society.

A simple example may help to illustrate this point. Suppose that society has already decided to spend $50 billion on public goods at the federal level. Suppose that the only public goods to be provided are defense and international affairs. How much should be spent on defense compared with international affairs? Clearly, the first thing to be identified is the goal to be achieved in each case. Once such goals are identified and their worth calculated, fewer dollars should

[7] Cost-benefit analysis has applicability, however, to other areas of federal spending such as education, health, and water projects. These activities fall under the category of semipublic goods, which will be discussed in the next section. See Robert Dorfman (ed.), *Measuring Benefits of Government Investments* (Brookings Institution, 1965).

be devoted to defense, for example, if some defense activities are worth less to society than the benefits derived from an equivalent amount of dollars spent on international affairs. The total budget— $50 billion—should be allocated between defense and international affairs in such a way that the benefit to society from the last dollar spent on both activities is equalized.

Is such a criterion feasible to apply? Here again the answer must be negative. In the area of public goods, economic criteria offer little guidance in determining the total level of federal spending and in choosing between alternative uses. As Walter Heller put it:

The economist recognizes, of course, that there are areas in which he is necessarily mute, or at least should not speak unless spoken to. These are the areas of pure public goods, whose benefits are clearly indivisible and nonmarketable, and no amount of economic wisdom can determine the appropriate levels of output and expenditure. In the realm of defense, for example, one successful Russian earth satellite or intercontinental ballistics missile will (and should) outweigh 10,000 economists in determining the appropriate level of expenditures.[8]

The final question—how should expenditures be allocated among alternative means of achieving a given goal—is less difficult to answer. In fact, this is the area where systems analysis, in particular cost-effectiveness analysis, has been successfully applied.[9] It was first introduced into the federal government in 1961 in the decision-making process in the Department of Defense. Since then, it has been embodied in the planning-programming-budgeting system (PPBS) and applied to all other federal programs. (See Chapter 3 for a discussion of PPBS.)

Cost-effectiveness is a method for evaluating the various means available to achieve the most for a given cost or a given objective for the least cost.[10] The application and usefulness of cost-effectiveness analysis can be illustrated by some examples in the area of defense.

Suppose that the decision maker is concerned with the allocation of the portion of the national defense budget earmarked for improv-

[8] Walter W. Heller, "Economics and the Applied Theory of Public Expenditures," in Joint Economic Committee, *Federal Expenditure Policy for Economic Growth and Stability,* 85 Cong. 1 sess. (1957), p. 103.

[9] Systems analysis is concerned with the discovery and specification of objectives and the evaluation of alternative means of reaching these objectives.

[10] Charles J. Hitch, *Decision-Making for Defense* (University of California Press, 1965), p. 43.

ing offensive forces, fixed at $A billion. He can use this amount for either the procurement of additional Minuteman missiles or additional Polaris submarines, and his objective will be to maximize the total offensive capability of the given budget. For each alternative force (Minuteman versus Polaris), a quantitative estimate of costs and expected military benefits (effectiveness) must thus be computed. Suppose that the effectiveness of each force can be measured by a single number—for example, the expected number of enemy that can be killed or targets destroyed. Then if all of the $A billion is spent on Minuteman squadrons, X number of enemy or targets will be the offensive capability, and on the other hand, if the $A billion is spent on Polaris submarines, Y number of enemy or targets will be the capability. A clear-cut choice can thus be made in favor of the Minuteman if X is greater than Y because that choice will maximize the effectiveness of the given defense budget.[11]

This example illustrates one aspect of cost-effectiveness, that is, obtaining the most output from a given budget. Consider another defense example, which illustrates how a given objective may be achieved with the least cost.[12] Suppose a defense objective is to be able to destroy 97 out of 100 enemy targets, using missiles each of which has a 50 percent chance of destroying a single target. That is, if 100 missiles are fired, 50 targets will be destroyed. If a second 100 are fired, 25 of the 50 targets left will be destroyed, or a total of 75. Firing 300 will destroy about 87 targets, 400 will destroy 94 targets, and 500 will destroy 97 targets. In this case, a 97 percent goal can be achieved at a minimum cost of 500 missiles.

An important aspect of cost-effectiveness analysis is that, although it makes the policy maker's choices explicit, it does not itself make the correct choice obvious. In the previous example, the first 100 missiles accomplish 50 kills, while the last 100 missiles increase the destruction capability by only 3 kills (from 94 kills to 97 kills). Does such a small increase in destructive capability justify the cost of the last 100 missiles? The defense decision maker must decide whether the additional output (3 kills) is worth the additional cost of the last 100 missiles. By bringing such information to his atten-

---

[11] For more detail, see Charles J. Hitch and Roland N. McKean, *The Economics of Defense in the Nuclear Age* (Harvard University Press, 1960), pp. 112–34; David Novick (ed.), *Program Budgeting—Program Analysis and the Federal Budget* (RAND Corporation, 1964), esp. Chap. 3.

[12] Hitch, *Decision-Making for Defense*, pp. 50–51.

tion, cost-effectiveness analysis can contribute a great deal to shaping the decision maker's judgment. In short, while not "making the decision," this method sorts out the factors which need to be taken into account in reaching a decision.

Spending on Semipublic Goods

Consider the federal expenditures grouped together in the second section of Table 12. This $15.1 billion represents expenditures on what may be called semipublic goods. This type of spending is relatively small at the federal level (accounting for less than 11 percent of federal expenditures in 1966), but it is a very large part of state and local government expenditures. Semipublic goods are goods and services that benefit individual users rather than society as a whole but that, in fact, benefit society through their effects on individuals. Take, for example, the case of education, which yields a direct benefit to the user in the form of a higher expected life income and an indirect benefit to society as a whole in the form of a better environment for innovations, better qualified voters, better health, a reduction in the crime rate, and so on. Such a semipublic good can be supplied by private producers in a free market economy, as in the case of private schools and colleges, but since education provides extra benefits to society, the government may be called upon to supplement the amount of education supplied by the private market.

Education as a semipublic good is provided mostly by state and local governments, in the form of public schools, colleges, and universities. The federal government, however, contributes to state and local government spending on education through its grants-in-aid. As Table 12 shows, 76 percent of federal spending on education is in that form. In addition, the federal government provides aid to education for areas affected by federal installations, loans and grants to college students, and other services. Various proposals have been made in recent years to extend federal aid to construction of school buildings, teachers' salaries, and other educational costs. Opinions on these proposals have generally revolved around the criteria of efficiency versus decentralization discussed earlier.

In order to determine how much the federal government should spend on the semipublic goods for which it, rather than state and local governments, has been given responsibility, the benefits accruing to the individual and to the community must both be identified and compared with their costs. Cost-benefit calculation—if it could be applied to all semipublic goods—would determine the aggregate level of federal spending in this area. Spending on semipublic goods would continue as long as the benefits to society exceeded the costs to society, or perhaps until they were equalized.

Benefit-cost calculations are often more feasible in the area of semipublic goods than in that of public goods. This technique in recent years has been applied in many areas, such as education, health, aviation, power projects, transportation, and water resources. However, lack of reliable statistical data, the difficulty of quantifying in certain cases, and the social elements of benefits and costs have prevented (at least for the present) its use in determining the total budget for semipublic goods. As it now stands, the level of spending is determined through the political process.

Allocation of a given budget among the various semipublic activities—education, health, transportation, and so on—can, however, be based on the cost-benefit criterion—at least to some extent. For those activities where quantification is possible, the costs and benefits to society of each activity can be calculated and the results compared. The budget then can be allocated to the activities in such a way that society's *net* benefits from an additional unit of spending on each activity are equal to the cost.[13]

Among semipublic goods, cost-benefit analysis is used to evaluate the merits of existing federal programs as well as proposals for new programs, thus providing the decision maker with some economic basis for judging which are worthwhile and which are not. A number of formulas for evaluating social benefits and social costs are in use. The choice of a formula depends on how the following basic issues are resolved: (1) Which costs and which benefits should be included? (2) How are they to be valued? (3) At what interest rate are they to be discounted?

[13] Cost-benefit analysis originated as an administrative device adapted to a strictly limited type of federal activity, namely, the improvement of navigation. The River and Harbor Act of 1902 required a board of engineers to study the desirability of Army Corps of Engineers' river and harbor projects in terms of the benefits to commerce and the cost. The Flood Control Act of 1936 is another example of the application of cost-benefit analysis to government projects. For early application of the concept, see R. J. Hammond, *Benefit-Cost Analysis and Water Pollution Control* (Stanford University, Ford Research Institute, 1960), and Dorfman (ed.), *Measuring Benefits of Government Investments*.

The importance of these points can be illustrated by the following example. Suppose that the federal program to be evaluated is designed to reduce the number of high-school dropouts.[14] The goal, then, is to determine whether or not, on the basis of the expected benefits and costs, the program is worthwhile. The starting point in any cost-benefit formula is a projection of the physical output, in this case, the number of dropouts prevented either in each year of the program or in some typical year of its operation. Next, the return (benefits) from dropout prevention must be estimated. Since dropout prevention—a semipublic good—yields benefits directly to the individual as well as to society as a whole, two types of benefits have to be estimated. The first type—the benefit to the individual—can be estimated fairly easily by computing the present value of additional lifetime income that the student may expect.[15] The benefit to society is more difficult to estimate since a dollar figure (with due allowance for discounting) must be assigned to the impact of dropout prevention on such factors as crime and delinquency, the unemployment rate, transfer payments (such as unemployment compensation), and tax revenues. Thus, for this program, only an approximate measure of society's benefits can be estimated.

After a dollar figure has been computed for the total benefit, a similar procedure must be followed to estimate the full cost of the program in terms of the actual resources that will be needed. The rest is simple—the benefits are the numerator, the costs are the denominator, and the result is the benefit-cost ratio. If this ratio is greater than one—that is, if benefits exceed costs—the program is worthwhile; otherwise it should not be undertaken. The benefit-cost ratio can thus be a valuable guide to policy. The higher the ratio, the greater the payoff. Alternative programs can be ranked according to their benefit-cost ratios to facilitate the decision maker's choice among them. Clearly, a program with a ratio of 9 is to be preferred to a program with a ratio of 4.

The danger of accepting without reservations the dollar magni-

[14] Burton A. Weisbrod, "Preventing High School Dropouts," in Dorfman (ed.), *Measuring Benefits of Government Investments*, pp. 117–67.

[15] To calculate the present value of future income a discount rate must be used, but there is no general agreement on the appropriate discount rate. For more detail, see A. R. Prest and R. Turvey, "Cost-Benefit Analysis: A Survey," *Economic Journal*, December 1965, pp. 683–735, and Samuel B. Chase, Jr. (ed.), *Problems in Public Expenditure Analysis* (Brookings Institution, 1968).

tudes produced by benefit-cost analyses cannot be overstressed. Serious difficulties are present in quantifying benefits as well as costs and in choosing the appropriate discount rate for alternative programs.[16]

Spending To Affect Income Distribution

Federal government spending and taxation also arise out of efforts to promote equity in the distribution of income among persons and regions. The federal expenditures in group 3 of Table 12 were designed primarily for this purpose. As can be seen from the table, this type of spending bulks very large in the federal budget. It represented some 30 percent of total expenditures in 1966, for example. In that year, of the $42.6 billion of federal spending on the items in group 3, $29.6 billion was in the form of transfer payments, $6.4 billion was for grants-in-aid to state and local governments (for public assistance, relief, and welfare), $4.7 billion was for subsidies (less the current surplus of government enterprises) and finally, $2.1 billion represented purchases of goods and services.

In our society, government spending and taxation affect the distribution of income in two ways. First, when government taxes and spends, it usually alters the distribution of income to some extent regardless of whether it had such an objective in mind. When, for example, a contract is awarded to a business firm to build submarines, the government's primary objective is a stronger defense posture. Nevertheless, this expenditure, and the way in which it is financed, probably will have some effect on the distribution of income. The business firm to which the contract is awarded, and also its suppliers of materials and labor, will benefit directly in terms of work opportunities, income, and profits.

The second way in which government spending and taxation affect the distribution of income is through programs specifically designed for that purpose. These are the activities listed in group 3 of Table 12. Federal spending on public housing, agriculture, public hospitals, medical services, old age and retirement benefits, veterans' benefits, and public assistance and relief is undertaken especially for the benefit of certain individuals or groups—mostly the poor, the aged, or those in distressed circumstances for economic or other rea-

[16] See Chase (ed.), *Problems in Public Expenditure Analysis, passim.*

sons. Although the benefit derived from this type of spending may accrue to all individuals in the society, the important point to note is that particular groups of individuals (the aged, the disabled, veterans, farmers, and so on) benefit more than others.

In this area as well as in the areas of public and semipublic goods, cost-effectiveness analysis may be performed to evaluate the relative merits of alternative programs that are designed to accomplish the same goal. For example, cost-effectiveness may be used to determine whether a negative income tax is superior or inferior to a public assistance program of the same magnitude in alleviating poverty.[17] It has also been argued that cost-benefit analysis can be used to evaluate the redistributional effects of federal programs.[18] However, this is a new area for this type of analysis, and its usefulness and feasibility are only now beginning to be demonstrated in practical applications to government programs.

Taxation may also be used specifically to redistribute income. For example, the government may design a tax structure (a combination of certain income, gift, death, and other taxes) to achieve this objective.[19]

It would probably be inaccurate to say that the executive branch or the majority of Congress has any carefully considered overall view of how income should be distributed. Nevertheless, decisions on specific proposals in the areas listed above all involve implicit judgments on a desirable distribution of income. Unanimity of opinion about what is "fair" or "equitable" may be impossible to attain, since "fairness" does not necessarily mean the same thing for everyone in our society or for every society at every moment in time. Specifically, what is considered unfair today may have been acceptable in earlier times. Nevertheless, some general distributional patterns are probably supported by a majority, and fairly widespread agreement is often reached on many specific cases.

[17] For an explanation of the negative income tax idea, see Joseph A. Pechman, *Federal Tax Policy* (Brookings Institution, 1966), pp. 72–75, and Christopher Greene, *Negative Taxes and the Poverty Problem* (Brookings Institution, 1967).

[18] Arthur Maass, "Benefit-Cost Analysis: Its Relevance to Public Investment Decisions," *Quarterly Journal of Economics,* May 1966, pp. 208–26; Burton A. Weisbrod, "Income Redistribution Effects and Cost-Benefit Analysis," in Chase (ed.), *Problems in Public Expenditure Analysis,* pp. 177–209.

[19] Alternatively, the government may interfere directly (not through spending or taxation) in the determination of income in the private market by imposing minimum wages or minimum prices for certain services or products.

Given a goal of a particular pattern of income distribution, the federal government will set transfers and taxes to achieve that goal. That is, given (1) the initial allocation of wealth and income generated by private markets and (2) the effects on distribution of federal spending and taxing for other purposes, such as the production of public goods, there will be a certain amount of government transfers and taxes required to achieve the desired pattern. The specific amount will depend on what the desired distribution is and how different it is from the existing distribution.

Other Federal Spending

The fourth group in Table 12 consists of net interest paid. In 1966, interest paid on its debt to the public by the federal government accounted for 6.6 percent of federal expenditures. Since the debt was incurred mostly as the result of past wars and recessions, it has something of the character of a defense expenditure or of an expenditure that represents in part the cost to the government of stabilizing the economy.

Some Common Fallacies in Judging Federal Spending

There are uncomfortably few criteria that can be used to determine the optimum level of federal expenditures and taxation because of the difficulty of measuring the benefits and costs of many government goods and services. One frequently heard argument against government spending is that by its very nature government is less efficient than the private sector in providing goods and services. Private firms, it is claimed, are relatively free of the bureaucratic red tape and political maneuvering that make for inefficiency. And since private production is carried on at closer to minimum feasible cost than public production, the production of goods and services should generally be left in private hands.

Whether government production of goods and services is in fact relatively inefficient might well be debated. And it is possible that profit maximization might not be the only incentive to efficiency. Efficiency aside, however, there are two weaknesses in this argument. One is that it confuses production with spending. Over half of federal spending on goods and services is for goods produced by private firms; most of the rest consists of payment for services of government employees. In other words, for the most part, government is not in competition with private industry. The second weakness in this argument is that there is no use showing that private producers are more efficient than the government if private producers are unable or unwilling to provide the goods or services in question. This is the case with police and fire protection, defense, public health services, and so on. In short, government spending on public goods is spending that cannot or will not be duplicated by the private sector. To eliminate defense spending because it is wastefully administered and to let people buy more cars instead resembles, as one observer put it, the action taken by a "man in Atlanta who wanted to go to New Orleans but decided to take the train to New York because it was faster."[20] This is not to say that we should be tolerant of waste in the administration of government programs. The lack of a profit incentive can make inefficiency a serious problem. But if these programs are meeting public wants, as expressed through the political process, then a demonstration of waste in the programs is an argument for eliminating waste, not for eliminating the programs. In fact, there has already been an effort in this direction, the planning-programming-budgeting system discussed in Chapter 3, which is specifically designed to raise efficiency in government programs. Programs are evaluated and compared in terms of their effectiveness so that society pays no more than is necessary to achieve a given governmental goal.

Another argument against government spending states that the taxes required to pay for government expenditures distort consumer and producer choices by causing the market prices of goods, as well as of the factors of production, to diverge from what they would have been in the absence of these taxes. This divergence, it is said, involves a dead-weight loss of efficiency in the production of private goods. The answer to this argument would again be that, though waste engendered by a bad tax system is real and significant, this is not an argument against federal spending. For if such expenditures were eliminated, as we have said before, the market economy would not itself provide the public goods or transfer payments. Taxes ought to be considered in estimating the benefits and costs of gov-

[20] Francis M. Bator, *The Question of Government Spending: Public Needs and Private Wants* (Harper & Row, 1960), p. 103.

ernment programs, but the existence of the cost of tax collection or any other burden of the tax structure does not mean that the program is not worthwhile but that the tax structure should be changed.

There are also some fallacies in the arguments commonly used to support more government spending. Quite often, for example, government expenditures are compared with GNP, and it is implied that in some sense a rise in government spending is justified by a rise in GNP or that government spending *should* rise in step with GNP. While such a comparison may provide a measure of the relative importance of government in the economy, it is no criterion for judging the desirable level of government expenditures. This should be gauged as far as possible on the basis of costs and benefits to society. At times, therefore, government spending need not grow as fast as GNP, and at other times, government spending should grow faster than GNP. The relation of government spending to GNP by itself does not provide a useful criterion for evaluating expenditures.

It is also misleading to judge federal expenditures solely with reference to fiscal policy. When there is unemployment, there may be strong pressure for increased spending. But all new or expanded programs must still be judged on efficiency grounds. There is usually no justification for make-work spending just to reduce unemployment. Tax cuts should be considered as an alternative, and where this is not feasible or is ineffective and increased spending is necessary for fiscal policy reasons, programs should be chosen in which the benefits exceed the costs. In short, more federal spending, even when there is unemployment, is not necessarily the best solution.

These examples of rules of thumb and the faulty reasoning behind each could be extended almost indefinitely. Statements like "when defense spending goes up, nondefense spending should go down by an equal amount," or "government spending is generally wasteful" reflect a misunderstanding of the function of government spending and taxation which, it is hoped, has been corrected at least to some extent by this book.

Summary

Federal expenditures arise from the public's desire for public and semipublic goods—those that are not provided at all, or are provided inadequately, by the private market—and from efforts to achieve equity in the distribution of income. There are no precise economic rules or guidelines for judging the proper amount of expenditure for each of these purposes. For some federal programs, however, particularly in the area of semipublic goods such as health, education, and natural resource development, an estimate of costs and benefits of projects can be of help in determining the proper amount of expenditure. For other programs, most particularly in the area of public goods such as defense, international affairs, and redistribution of income, cost-benefit analysis cannot readily be applied to answer the question of how much the federal government should spend. In the latter cases, federal expenditure policy turns largely on the citizenry's preferences for federal versus state and local responsibility, public versus private goods, and the degree of redistribution of income. After programs have been chosen through the political process, however, and the total level of spending decided upon, cost-benefit and cost-effectiveness analysis can often guide the policy maker in choosing among alternative programs—in evaluating the relative merits of new as well as existing programs. This is the purpose of the planning-programming-budgeting system, which has recently been adopted throughout the federal government.

APPENDIXES

Appendix A.   Statistical Tables

Appendix B.   Bibliographical Notes

Table A-1. Budget Receipts, Outlays, Financing, and Debt, 1958–67

(In millions of dollars)

Budget item	1958	1959	1960	1961	1962	1963	1964	1965	1966	1967
Receipts, expenditures, and net lending										
Expenditure account										
Receipts	79,617	79,048	92,481	94,393	99,656	106,578	112,702	116,855	130,901	149,391
Expenditures (excludes net lending)	81,177	89,693	90,385	96,717	104,660	111,465	118,122	116,718	130,740	153,238
Expenditure deficit	−1,560	−10,645	2,096	−2,324	−5,004	−4,887	−5,420	137	161	−3,637
Loan account										
Loan disbursements	6,520	7,859	8,310	7,869	9,621	9,646	10,237	10,911	14,628	17,787
Loan repayments	4,976	5,201	6,427	6,671	7,271	9,791	9,693	9,662	10,796	12,611
Net lending	1,544	2,659	1,882	1,198	2,351	−145	545	1,249	3,832	5,176
Total budget										
Receipts	79,617	79,048	92,481	94,393	99,656	106,578	112,702	116,855	130,901	149,591
Expenditures and net lending	82,720	92,352	92,268	97,915	107,011	111,320	118,667	117,966	134,572	158,414
Budget deficit	−3,103	−13,304	213	−3,522	−7,355	−4,742	−5,965	−1,111	−3,671	−8,823
Budget financing[a]										
Borrowing from the public	6,607	8,331	1,777	1,143	9,453	5,971	2,978	3,953	6,031	3,551
Reduction in cash balances, and so on	−3,504	4,973	−1,990	2,379	−2,098	−1,229	2,987	−2,842	−2,360	5,272
Total budget financing	3,103	13,304	−213	3,522	7,355	4,742	5,965	1,111	3,671	8,823
Outstanding debt at end of year[a]										
Gross amount outstanding	279,147	286,666	289,243	290,991	301,074	308,488	314,377	320,806	329,473	341,343
Held by the public	225,972	234,303	236,080	237,223	246,676	252,647	255,625	259,578	265,609	269,160

Source: U.S. Bureau of the Budget, *The Budget of the United States Government, Fiscal Year 1969* (1968), p. 538.

[a] Data represent results of preliminary adjustment to new budget concepts and may be revised later.

147

Table A-2. Budget Receipts by Source, 1958–67

(In millions of dollars)

Source of revenue	1958	1959	1960	1961	1962	1963	1964	1965	1966	1967
Individual income taxes	34,724	36,719	40,715	41,338	45,571	47,588	48,697	48,792	55,446	61,526
Corporation income taxes	20,074	17,309	21,494	20,955	20,523	21,579	23,492	25,461	30,073	33,971
Employment taxes	8,624	8,821	11,248	12,679	12,835	14,746	16,959	17,358	20,662	27,823
Unemployment insurance	1,924	2,131	2,668	2,904	3,337	4,112	4,045	3,819	3,777	3,652
Premiums for insurance and retirement	682	769	768	866	873	944	1,006	1,079	1,126	1,853
Excise taxes	10,638	10,578	11,676	11,860	12,534	13,194	13,731	14,570	13,061	13,719
Estate and gift taxes	1,393	1,333	1,606	1,896	2,016	2,167	2,394	2,716	3,066	2,978
Customs	781	925	1,105	982	1,142	1,206	1,252	1,442	1,767	1,901
Other receipts	777	463	1,200	913	825	1,042	1,126	1,617	1,923	2,168
Total budget receipts	79,617	79,048	92,481	94,393	99,656	106,578	112,702	116,855	130,901	149,591
Interfund and intragovernmental transactions, and proprietary receipts from the public[a]	4,119	5,330	5,309	6,508	5,654	7,099	6,655	6,761	7,592	11,536[b]

Source: *Budget for Fiscal Year 1969*, p. 539.
[a] Excluded above; offset against expenditures.
[b] Interfund and intragovernmental transactions—6,588; proprietary receipts from the public—4,948.

148

Table A-3. Budget Outlays by Function, 1958–67

(In millions of dollars)

Type of expenditure	1958	1959	1960	1961	1962	1963	1964	1965	1966	1967
					Year					
Expenditures										
National defense	44,461	46,667	45,848	47,532	51,179	52,275	53,682	49,586	56,771	70,095
International affairs and finance	2,912	2,790	3,310	3,242	4,034	4,279	4,434	4,196	4,343	4,110
Space research and technology	89	145	401	744	1,257	2,252	4,171	5,091	5,932	5,424
Agriculture and agricultural resources	2,541	4,718	2,893	2,877	3,491	4,398	4,545	4,032	2,764	3,156
Natural resources	1,203	1,233	1,084	1,626	1,736	1,607	2,042	2,140	2,167	2,113
Commerce and transportation	2,922	4,367	4,643	4,929	5,193	5,516	6,283	7,043	6,789	7,308
Housing and community development	-36	30	21	157	160	193	151	116	442	578
Health, labor, and welfare	15,763	18,019	19,105	22,368	23,963	25,677	27,201	28,143	33,194	39,512
Education	375	550	659	740	842	953	1,109	1,309	2,449	3,602
Veterans' benefits and services	5,076	5,183	5,063	5,392	5,378	5,666	5,552	5,634	5,707	6,366
Interest	6,936	7,070	8,299	8,108	8,321	9,215	9,810	10,358	11,285	12,548
General government	1,010	1,159	1,332	1,508	1,653	1,799	2,072	2,231	2,316	2,452
Special allowances	—	—	—	—	—	—	—	—	—	—
Undistributed adjustments to amounts above	-2,076	-2,239	-2,272	-2,506	-2,547	-2,666	-2,931	-3,164	-3,421	-4,022
Total expenditures	81,177	89,693	90,385	96,717	104,660	111,465	118,122	116,715	130,740	153,238
Net lending										
National defense	1	-12	-7	-41	[a]	-64	-31	-3	-1	-3
International affairs and finance	433	418	-235	127	528	-95	-283	-21	100	540
Agriculture and agricultural resources	472	700	457	462	648	731	642	777	911	1,221
Natural resources	3	6	11	18	21	16	23	16	19	19
Commerce and transportation	56	71	27	74	193	145	139	275	193	138
Housing and community development	165	1,064	1,078	64	490	-1,012	-301	-147	1,984	1,708
Health, labor, and welfare	—	—	—	[a]	1	3	2	19	32	572
Education	165	180	204	201	231	288	225	229	376	445
Veterans' benefits and services	261	245	363	296	248	-146	129	88	214	532
General government	-12	-14	-15	-3	-8	-11	-1	16	5	2
Total net lending	1,544	2,659	1,882	1,198	2,351	-145	545	1,249	3,832	5,176
Total expenditures and net lending	82,720	92,352	92,268	97,915	107,011	111,320	118,667	117,966	134,572	158,414

Source: *Budget for Fiscal Year 1969*, p. 540.

[a] Less than $500 thousand.

Table A-4. Federal Receipts from the Public by Source, 1934-67 [a]

(In millions of dollars)

Fiscal year	Individual income taxes	Corporation income taxes	Excise taxes	Employment taxes	Estate and gift taxes	Customs	Unemployment insurance deposits	Veterans insurance premiums	Other	Total [b]
1934	410	393	1,691	—	110	299	—	66	157	3,126
1935	512	572	1,934	—	211	322	—	63	209	3,823
1936	666	746	1,693	—	376	371	19	64	219	4,154
1937	1,066	1,073	1,857	252	303	471	292	63	259	5,636
1938	1,287	1,328	1,864	714	413	342	748	63	281	7,040
1939	1,022	1,138	1,861	739	357	302	811	63	271	6,564
1940	959	1,123	1,937	836	357	331	860	60	380	6,879
1941	1,400	2,029	2,555	929	403	365	892	61	568	9,202
1942	3,205	4,727	3,393	1,191	421	369	1,096	102	600	15,104
1943	6,490	9,570	4,093	1,505	442	308	1,218	335	1,136	25,097
1944	19,701	14,737	4,761	1,747	507	417	1,349	836	3,763	47,818
1945	18,415	15,146	6,267	1,785	638	341	1,256	1,012	5,302	50,162
1946	16,157	11,833	6,999	1,707	669	424	1,010	903	3,835	43,537
1947	17,835	8,569	7,207	2,030	770	477	1,005	571	5,067	43,531
1948	19,305	9,678	7,356	2,388	890	403	1,007	434	3,895	45,357
1949	15,548	11,195	7,502	2,476	780	367	985	431	2,293	41,576
1950	15,745	10,448	7,549	2,881	698	407	1,098	440	1,673	40,940
1951	21,643	14,106	8,648	3,928	708	609	1,363	520	1,865	53,390
1952	27,913	21,225	8,851	4,563	818	533	1,439	473	2,197	68,013
1953	30,108	21,238	9,868	4,980	881	596	1,371	428	2,028	71,499
1954	29,542	21,101	9,945	5,382	934	542	1,246	426	2,508	71,626
1955	28,747	17,861	9,131	6,166	924	585	1,146	441	2,834	67,836
1956	32,188	20,880	9,929	7,228	1,161	682	1,330	441	3,249	77,087
1957	35,620	21,167	10,534	7,520	1,365	735	1,542	452	3,171	82,105
1958	34,724	20,074	10,638	8,565	1,393	782	1,501	485	3,730	81,892
1959	36,719	17,309	10,578	8,767	1,333	925	1,701	478	3,851	81,660
1960	40,715	21,494	11,676	11,067	1,606	1,105	2,167	482	4,766	95,078
1961	41,338	20,954	11,860	12,405	1,896	982	2,398	504	4,905	97,242
1962	45,571	20,523	12,534	12,561	2,015	1,142	2,729	501	4,288	101,865
1963	47,588	21,579	13,194	14,862	2,167	1,206	3,009	494	5,641	109,739
1964	48,697	23,493	13,731	16,832	2,394	1,252	3,042	494	5,596	115,530
1965	48,792	25,461	14,570	16,905	2,716	1,442	3,052	488	6,274	119,699
1966	55,446	30,073	13,062	20,022	3,066	1,767	3,067	511	7,466	134,480
1967	61,526	33,971	13,719	n.a.	2,978	1,901	n.a.	n.a.	n.a.	153,596

Sources: Data for 1954-63 are from U.S. Bureau of the Budget, The Budget of the United States Government, The Budget of the United States Government, Fiscal Year 1965 (1964), p. 462; data for 1964-66 are from The Budget of the United States Government, . . . 1968 (1967), p. 467; data for other years were obtained directly from the Bureau of the Budget and the U.S. Treasury Department. The last may differ slightly from published figures because of adjustments in the functional categories.   n.a. Not available.

[a] Receipts are net after refunds.

[b] Totals from 1934 through 1941 may not be precise to the level of significance shown because adjustments were for major intragovernmental transactions only.

150

Table A-5. Distribution of Federal Receipts from the Public by Source, 1934–67

(In percent)

Fiscal year	Indi- vidual income taxes	Corpo- ration income taxes	Excise taxes	Employ- ment taxes	Estate and gift taxes	Cus- toms	Unem- ploy- ment insur- ance deposits	Veter- ans' insur- ance pre- miums	Other
1934	13.1	12.6	54.1	—	3.5	9.6	—	2.1	5.0
1935	13.4	15.0	50.6	—	5.5	8.4	—	1.6	5.5
1936	16.0	18.0	40.8	—	9.1	8.9	0.5	1.5	5.3
1937	18.9	19.0	32.9	4.5	5.4	8.4	5.2	1.1	4.6
1938	18.3	18.9	26.5	10.1	5.9	4.9	10.6	0.9	4.0
1939	15.6	17.3	28.4	11.3	5.4	4.6	12.4	1.0	4.1
1940	13.9	16.3	28.2	12.2	5.2	4.8	12.5	0.9	5.5
1941	15.2	22.0	27.8	10.1	4.4	4.0	9.7	0.7	6.2
1942	21.2	31.3	22.5	7.9	2.8	2.4	7.3	0.7	4.0
1943	25.9	38.1	16.3	6.0	1.8	1.2	4.9	1.3	4.5
1944	41.2	30.8	10.0	3.7	1.1	0.9	2.8	1.7	7.9
1945	36.7	30.2	12.5	3.6	1.3	0.7	2.5	2.0	10.6
1946	37.1	27.2	16.1	3.9	1.5	1.0	2.3	2.1	8.8
1947	41.0	19.7	16.6	4.7	1.8	1.1	2.3	1.3	11.6
1948	42.6	21.3	16.2	5.3	2.0	0.9	2.2	1.0	8.6
1949	37.4	26.9	18.0	6.0	1.9	0.9	2.4	1.0	5.5
1950	38.5	25.5	18.4	7.0	1.7	1.0	2.7	1.1	4.1
1951	40.5	26.4	16.2	7.4	1.3	1.1	2.6	1.0	3.5
1952	41.0	31.2	13.0	6.7	1.2	0.8	2.1	0.7	3.3
1953	42.1	29.7	13.8	7.0	1.2	0.8	2.0	0.6	2.9
1954	41.2	29.5	13.9	7.5	1.3	0.8	1.7	0.6	3.5
1955	42.4	26.3	13.5	9.1	1.4	0.9	1.7	0.7	4.2
1956	41.8	27.1	12.9	9.4	1.5	0.9	1.7	0.6	4.2
1957	43.4	25.8	12.8	9.2	1.7	0.9	1.9	0.6	3.9
1958	42.4	24.5	13.0	10.5	1.7	1.0	1.8	0.6	4.6
1959	45.0	21.2	13.0	10.7	1.6	1.1	2.1	0.6	4.7
1960	42.8	22.6	12.3	11.6	1.7	1.2	2.3	0.5	5.0
1961	42.5	21.5	12.2	12.8	1.9	1.0	2.5	0.5	5.0
1962	44.7	20.1	12.3	12.3	2.0	1.1	2.7	0.5	4.2
1963	43.4	19.7	12.0	13.5	2.0	1.1	2.7	0.5	5.1
1964	42.2	20.3	11.9	14.6	2.1	1.1	2.6	0.4	4.8
1965	40.8	21.8	12.2	14.1	2.3	1.2	2.5	0.4	5.2
1966	41.2	22.4	9.7	14.9	2.3	1.3	2.3	0.4	5.6
1967	40.1	22.1	8.9	n.a.	1.9	1.2	n.a.	n.a.	n.a.

Source: Table A-4. Percentages may not add to 100.0 because of rounding.
n.a. Not available.

Table A-6. Federal Payments to the Public by Function, 1948–67

(In millions of dollars)

Fiscal year	National defense	International affairs and finance[a]	Agriculture and agricultural resources	Veterans' benefits and services	Interest	Health, labor, and welfare	Other	Total[b]
1948	13,015	5,554	559	6,897	3,909	3,035	3,492	36,493
1949	13,097	6,232	2,537	7,032	3,977	3,860	3,835	40,570
1950	13,121	4,596	2,858	9,277	4,315	5,100	3,880	43,147
1951	22,649	3,795	656	6,050	4,134	4,866	3,647	45,797
1952	44,243	2,946	1,155	5,823	4,134	5,666	3,995	67,962
1953	50,586	2,217	2,967	4,953	4,706	6,544	4,796	76,769
1954	47,138	1,696	2,617	5,042	4,620	8,083	2,662	71,858
1955	40,852	2,044	4,399	5,114	4,664	9,485	3,979	70,537
1956	40,854	1,624	4,977	5,328	5,115	10,254	4,394	72,546
1957	43,442	2,637	4,627	5,448	5,266	12,108	6,478	80,006
1958	44,552	2,651	4,347	5,828	5,884	15,757	4,453	83,472
1959	46,673	2,398	7,052	5,910	5,350	18,017	9,352	94,752
1960	45,915	1,574	4,877	5,907	7,233	19,107	9,715	94,328
1961	47,685	2,153	5,183	6,187	7,257	22,364	8,713	99,542
1962	51,462	2,492	5,492	6,092	6,940	23,975	10,759	107,662
1963	53,429	2,242	7,266	5,971	7,427	25,698	11,718	113,751
1964	54,514	3,837	5,416	6,107	8,011	27,191	15,076	120,332
1965	50,790	4,794	5,142	6,080	8,605	28,191	18,782	122,395
1966	58,464	4,463	4,114	5,556	9,215	33,249	22,756	137,817
1967	71,843	4,413	4,159	6,978	10,371	39,002	20,254	155,142

Source: See sources for Table A-4.

[a] Beginning in 1964, expenditures under the Food for Peace program are included in "international affairs and finance." Prior to that date, they were included in "agriculture."

[b] Includes technical adjustments not allocated by function.

Table A-7. Distribution of Federal Payments to the Public by Function, 1948–67

(In percent)

Fiscal year	National defense	Inter- national affairs and finance	Agriculture and agricultural resources	Veterans' benefits and services	Interest	Health, labor, and welfare	Other
1948	35.7	15.2	1.5	18.9	10.7	8.4	9.6
1949	32.3	15.4	6.3	17.3	9.8	9.5	9.5
1950	30.4	10.7	6.6	21.5	10.0	11.8	9.0
1951	49.5	8.3	1.4	13.2	9.0	10.6	8.0
1952	65.1	4.3	1.7	8.6	6.1	8.3	5.9
1953	65.9	2.9	3.9	6.5	6.1	8.5	6.2
1954	65.6	2.4	3.6	7.0	6.4	11.2	3.7
1955	58.0	3.0	6.2	7.2	6.6	13.4	5.6
1956	56.3	2.2	7.0	7.3	7.0	14.1	6.1
1957	54.3	3.3	5.8	6.8	6.6	15.1	8.1
1958	53.4	3.2	5.2	7.0	7.0	18.9	5.3
1959	49.3	2.5	7.4	6.2	5.6	19.0	10.0
1960	48.6	1.7	5.2	6.3	7.7	20.3	10.3
1961	47.9	2.2	5.2	6.2	7.3	22.5	8.8
1962	47.8	2.3	5.1	5.7	6.4	22.3	10.0
1963	47.0	2.0	6.4	5.2	6.5	22.6	10.3
1964	45.3	3.2	4.5	5.1	6.7	22.6	12.5
1965	41.5	3.9	4.2	5.0	7.0	23.0	15.3
1966	42.4	3.2	3.0	4.0	6.7	24.1	16.5
1967	46.3	2.8	2.7	4.5	6.7	25.1	13.1

Source: Table A-6. Percentages may not add to 100.0 because of rounding.

Table A-8. Federal Receipts by Type in the National Income Accounts, 1929-66

(In millions of dollars)

Calendar year	Personal tax and nontax receipts					Corporate profit tax accruals	Indirect business tax and nontax accruals					Contributions for social insurance
	Total	Income taxes	Estate and gift taxes	Non-taxes	Minus refunds		Total	Excise taxes	Customs duties	Non-taxes	Minus refunds	
1929	1,263	1,238	61	24	60	1,224	1,193	564	599	56	26	124
1930	1,134	1,093	56	29	49	744	1,045	537	474	56	22	124
1931	607	567	56	20	36	423	894	490	373	49	18	123
1932	331	320	30	16	35	328	924	635	259	43	13	125
1933	474	375	69	16	21	462	1,619	1,246	296	36	39	115
1934	595	452	129	13	14	644	2,181	1,833	308	37	89	121
1935	827	580	248	14	15	820	2,181	1,730	371	39	54	136
1936	1,130	740	386	17	13	1,252	2,251	1,693	403	39	22	391
1937	1,723	1,319	402	21	19	1,337	2,406	1,775	469	42	19	1,573
1938	1,635	1,244	390	20	19	895	2,216	1,709	357	45	22	1,734
1939	1,235	874	371	15	25	1,285	2,322	1,826	344	44	25	1,879
1940	1,364	1,036	341	16	29	2,635	2,627	2,122	327	46	35	2,015
1941	2,016	1,622	401	21	28	7,333	3,567	2,817	439	55	26	2,504
1942	4,668	4,062	471	42	28	11,065	4,049	3,364	313	67	24	3,161
1943	16,517	15,923	461	79	23	13,616	4,944	4,076	410	112	35	4,181
1944	17,536	17,133	565	108	344	12,484	6,171	5,257	378	219	55	4,817
1945	19,379	19,848	663	118	1,331	10,234	7,128	6,214	397	216	52	5,754
1946	17,166	17,987	734	97	1,653	8,642	7,791	7,267	503	100	79	5,493
1947	19,643	20,446	830	40	1,673	10,664	7,791	7,297	436	127	69	5,108
1948	18,973	19,825	900	34	1,786	11,847	7,970	7,501	410	142	83	4,511
1949	16,137	17,716	754	35	2,368	9,803	8,020	7,561	381	150	72	4,937

154

Year												
1950	18,090	19,108	659	32	1709	17,000	8,860	8,252	549	126	67	5,907
1951	26,131	27,134	751	46	1,800	21,452	9,352	8,677	591	152	68	7,085
1952	31,031	32,264	850	53	2,136	18,540	10,296	9,622	582	160	68	7,378
1953	32,247	33,878	922	64	2,617	19,457	10,895	10,215	589	173	82	7,369
1954	28,998	30,914	921	63	2,900	16,955	9,733	9,048	565	208	88	8,112
1955	31,437	33,505	982	50	3,100	20,648	10,674	9,866	679	225	96	9,327
1956	35,170	37,084	1,281	55	3,250	20,624	11,245	10,370	743	257	125	10,569
1957	37,411	39,436	1,448	45	3,518	20,183	11,793	10,926	787	271	191	12,242
1958	36,786	39,307	1,350	47	3,918	18,041	11,498	10,562	846	276	186	12,355
1959	39,900	42,620	1,426	44	4,190	22,454	12,544	11,370	1,080	300	206	14,843
1960	43,634	46,222	1,782	44	4,414	21,726	13,451	12,248	1,079	349	225	17,667
1961	44,685	47,572	1,972	45	4,904	21,751	13,603	12,376	1,077	396	246	18,235
1962	48,609	51,720	2,076	52	5,239	22,746	14,575	13,154	1,213	454	246	20,520
1963	51,471	54,882	2,264	57	5,732	24,640	15,318	13,771	1,283	523	259	23,091
1964	48,604	52,089	2,595	58	6,138	26,440	16,148	14,375	1,328	699	254	23,845
1965	53,806	56,029	2,849	52	5,124	29,305	16,523	14,089	1,706	996	268	25,183
1966	61,738	64,795	3,080	54	6,191	32,276	15,904	13,187	1,955	1,103	341	33,280

Sources: U.S. Department of Commerce, Office of Business Economics, The National Income and Product Accounts of the United States, 1929–1965 (1966), pp. 52–53, and Survey of Current Business, Vol. 47 (July 1967), p. 24.

Table A-9. Federal Expenditures by Type in the National Income Accounts, 1929–66

(In millions of dollars)

Calendar year	Purchases of goods and services			Transfer payments		Grants-in-aid to state and local governments	Net interest
	Compensation of employees	Structures	Other purchases	To persons	To foreigners		
1929	879	150	232	691	34	117	441
1930	915	203	254	735	36	125	380
1931	921	263	311	1,716	40	313	444
1932	880	323	253	931	21	134	479
1933	1,164	336	500	698	17	502	517
1934	1,694	413	874	600	10	1,633	590
1935	1,768	467	684	634	20	1,706	526
1936	3,570	646	719	2,064	32	724	485
1937	3,013	696	955	828	60	764	616
1938	3,505	632	1,272	1,196	29	778	619
1939	3,414	502	1,189	1,240	27	988	643
1940	3,489	813	1,713	1,421	32	857	726
1941	5,027	3,433	8,422	1,369	−14	807	774
1942	10,645	8,968	32,262	1,419	90	888	1,038
1943	20,899	5,312	54,937	1,239	−53	942	1,707
1944	27,250	2,359	59,393	1,841	−88	947	2,420
1945	29,786	1,530	42,863	4,310	352	870	3,334
1946	14,606	202	2,426	9,182	2,249	1,108	4,173
1947	9,395	405	2,744	8,827	1,943	1,738	4,169
1948	8,936	918	6,661	7,619	3,828	1,986	4,267
1949	10,027	1,332	8,753	8,727	5,106	2,228	4,403
1950	10,760	1,498	6,145	10,816	3,563	2,343	4,514
1951	16,256	2,853	18,543	8,531	3,106	2,487	4,713
1952	18,925	3,993	28,861	8,779	2,088	2,646	4,739
1953	18,614	3,936	34,484	9,454	1,978	2,834	4,858
1954	17,805	3,228	26,344	11,508	1,776	2,913	5,009
1955	18,387	2,332	23,371	12,412	2,042	3,120	4,928
1956	19,011	2,571	24,004	13,361	1,868	3,331	5,273
1957	19,608	2,934	26,996	15,718	1,775	4,209	5,694
1958	20,591	3,550	29,453	19,528	1,798	5,641	5,609
1959	21,030	3,565	29,064	20,086	1,849	6,827	6,433
1960	21,868	3,501	28,162	21,520	1,878	6,521	7,081
1961	22,925	3,857	30,626	24,948	2,089	7,241	6,624
1962	24,277	3,879	35,233	25,538	2,164	8,000	7,186
1963	25,261	3,762	35,221	26,961	2,179	9,143	7,740
1964	27,148	3,653	34,365	27,767	2,165	10,431	8,321
1965	28,459	3,689	34,625	30,265	2,166	11,158	8,698
1966	32,665	3,614	40,755	33,734	2,278	14,821	9,542

Sources: See sources for Table A-8.

Table A-10. Federal Expenditures by Function in the National Income Accounts, 1952–66[a]

(In millions of dollars)

Calendar year	Total	National defense	International affairs and finance	Education	Health, labor, and welfare	Veterans' benefits and services	Commerce, transportation, and housing	Agriculture	Space	Natural resources	General government
					Total expenditures						
1952	66,446	46,745	2,380	323	5,848	4,997	1,954	1,267	—	1,205	1,727
1953	72,297	49,428	2,216	362	6,753	4,742	1,679	4,178	—	1,265	1,674
1954	64,932	41,974	1,989	391	8,708	4,789	1,485	2,925	—	1,047	1,624
1955	63,346	39,362	2,264	398	9,276	5,027	1,476	2,909	—	807	1,827
1956	66,633	41,113	2,147	379	10,606	5,153	2,146	2,169	—	966	1,954
1957	73,886	45,015	2,076	453	13,038	5,343	2,682	2,254	—	1,133	1,892
1958	83,446	46,725	2,153	576	16,818	5,615	4,006	4,219	30	1,323	1,981
1959	84,639	46,904	2,228	642	17,558	5,639	4,877	3,014	263	1,354	2,160
1960	86,173	45,885	2,233	689	19,079	5,668	4,844	3,189	574	1,364	2,648
1961	95,720	48,896	2,530	770	22,730	6,143	5,460	3,980	893	1,617	2,701
1962	103,397	52,787	2,585	892	23,973	5,954	5,914	4,694	1,796	1,757	3,045
1963	106,482	52,130	2,611	1,014	25,311	6,210	6,544	4,037	3,370	1,851	3,404
1964	109,766	51,566	2,648	1,151	26,332	6,141	7,491	4,506	4,629	1,898	3,404
1965	114,700	51,789	2,650	1,274	29,520	6,362	7,223	4,534	5,592	2,036	3,720
1966	133,349	62,303	2,861	3,401	33,826	6,392	8,064	4,063	5,947	2,397	4,095

Footnotes to table appear on p. 160.

Table A-10—Continued

Calendar year	Total	National defense	International affairs and finance	Education	Health, labor, and welfare	Veterans' benefits and services	Commerce, transportation, and housing	Agriculture	Space	Natural resources	General government
					Purchases of goods and services						
1952	51,919	45,928	292	92	352	1,203	756	702	—	1,194	1,400
1953	57,200	48,664	236	106	387	1,097	581	3,610	—	1,276	1,243
1954	47,590	41,198	212	133	428	949	525	1,852	—	1,084	1,209
1955	44,270	38,557	221	137	366	955	277	1,624	—	853	1,280
1956	45,626	40,330	242	129	761	979	713	64	—	1,007	1,401
1957	49,550	44,225	300	177	782	1,011	810	−183	—	1,176	1,252
1958	53,779	45,902	353	232	764	1,084	933	1,853	30	1,371	1,257
1959	53,743	46,049	376	231	821	1,123	1,153	1,031	262	1,381	1,316
1960	53,769	44,946	348	231	899	1,183	1,550	944	572	1,393	1,703
1961	57,666	47,825	432	261	1,258	1,290	1,734	630	890	1,667	1,679
1962	63,716	51,582	410	319	1,545	1,343	1,887	1,141	1,785	1,794	1,910
1963	64,609	50,760	425	374	1,629	1,370	2,080	606	3,351	1,891	2,123
1964	65,174	49,992	477	428	1,666	1,450	2,196	435	4,606	1,955	1,969
1965	66,797	50,080	478	430	2,080	1,445	2,114	373	5,562	2,058	2,177
1966	77,070	60,498	569	448	2,331	1,520	2,375	−1,084	5,913	2,319	2,181
					Transfer payments						
1952	10,867	853	2,088	32	3,849	3,678	—	—	—	—	367
1953	11,432	777	1,978	16	4,602	3,586	—	—	—	—	473
1954	13,284	770	1,776	12	6,470	3,810	—	—	—	—	446
1955	14,454	787	2,042	10	7,073	4,052	—	—	—	—	490

Year											
1956	589	—	—	—	—	4,151	7,876	10	1,868	735	15,229
1957	677	—	—	—	—	4,322	10,007	10	1,775	702	17,493
1958	765	—	—	—	—	4,523	13,510	18	1,798	712	21,326
1959	880	—	—	—	—	4,509	13,947	27	1,849	723	21,935
1960	968	—	—	—	—	4,477	15,255	46	1,882	770	23,398
1961	1,042	—	—	—	—	4,844	18,131	62	2,092	866	27,037
1962	1,151	—	—	—	3	4,603	18,740	77	2,166	962	27,702
1963	1,300	—	—	—	12	4,831	19,626	88	2,179	1,104	29,140
1964	1,421	—	—	—	33	4,683	20,263	80	2,165	1,287	29,932
1965	1,557	—	—	—	14	4,907	22,253	106	2,166	1,428	32,431
1966	1,917	4	—	—	6	4,862	25,101	323	2,286	1,513	36,012

Grants-in-aid to state and local governments

Year											
1952	11	58	—	45	498	116	1,645	199	—	74	2,646
1953	12	66	—	46	577	59	1,739	240	—	95	2,834
1954	22	74	—	51	597	30	1,789	246	—	104	2,913
1955	20	79	—	60	750	20	1,838	251	—	102	3,120
1956	23	87	—	71	807	16	1,964	240	—	123	3,331
1957	23	98	—	81	1,319	8	2,244	266	—	170	4,209
1958	23	102	—	88	2,353	8	2,540	326	—	201	5,641
1959	32	117	1	123	3,152	8	2,787	384	—	223	6,827
1960	34	130	2	96	2,658	10	2,923	411	1	256	6,521
1961	36	119	3	103	2,885	10	3,339	446	4	296	7,241
1962	33	137	11	128	3,145	9	3,688	495	7	347	8,000
1963	33	148	19	122	3,826	9	4,056	551	6	373	9,143
1964	62	161	23	142	4,584	8	4,403	642	5	401	10,431
1965	46	193	30	156	4,395	10	5,187	737	5	399	11,158
1966	59	291	34	189	4,787	11	6,390	2,629	5	426	14,821

159

Table A-10—Continued

Calendar year	Total	National defense	International affairs and finance	Educa-tion	Health, labor, and welfare	Veterans' benefits and services	Commerce, transpor-tation, and housing	Agricul-ture	Space	Natural resources	General govern-ment
					Subsidies less current surplus of government interests						
1952	1,014	−110	—	—	2	—	700	520	—	−47	−51
1953	831	−108	2	—	25	—	521	522	—	−77	−54
1954	1,145	−98	1	—	21	—	363	1,022	—	−111	−53
1955	1,502	−84	1	—	−1	—	449	1,225	—	−125	37
1956	2,447	−75	37	—	5	7	626	2,034	—	−128	−59
1957	2,634	−82	1	—	5	2	553	2,356	—	−141	−60
1958	2,700	−90	2	—	4	—	720	2,278	—	−150	−64
1959	2,134	−91	3	—	3	−1	572	1,860	—	−144	−68
1960	2,485	−87	2	1	2	−2	636	2,149	—	−159	−57
1961	3,776	−91	2	1	2	−1	841	3,247	—	−169	−56
1962	3,979	−104	2	1	—	−1	879	3,425	—	−174	−49
1963	3,590	−107	1	1	—	—	626	3,309	—	−188	−52
1964	4,229	−114	1	1	—	—	678	3,929	—	−218	−48
1965	4,314	−118	1	1	—	—	700	4,005	—	−215	−60
1966	5,446	−134	1	1	4	−1	896	4,958	—	−217	−62

Sources: U.S. Department of Commerce, The National Income and Product Accounts of the United States, 1929–1965, pp. 60–67, and Survey of Current Business, Vol. 47 (July 1967) pp. 28–29.
ᵃ Excludes net interest paid by general government.

Table A-11. Federal Surpluses or Deficits in the Unified Budget, the Administrative Budget, the Cash Budget, and the National Income Accounts, 1932–67

(In billions of dollars)

Fiscal year	Surplus (+) or deficit (−)			
	Unified budget	Administrative budget	Cash budget	National income accounts[a]
1932	n.a.	− 2.7	− 2.8	− 1.5
1933	n.a.	− 2.6	− 2.6	− 1.3
1934	n.a.	− 3.6	− 3.4	− 2.9
1935	n.a.	− 2.8	− 2.5	− 2.6
1936	n.a.	− 4.4	− 3.4	− 3.5
1937	n.a.	− 2.8	− 2.8	− 0.2
1938	n.a.	− 1.2	− 0.2	− 2.0
1939	n.a.	− 3.9	− 2.8	− 2.2
1940	n.a.	− 3.9	− 2.7	− 1.5
1941	n.a.	− 6.2	− 4.8	− 1.3
1942	n.a.	−21.5	−19.4	−14.0
1943	n.a.	−57.4	−53.8	−47.9
1944	n.a.	−51.4	−46.1	−48.1
1945	n.a.	−53.9	−45.0	−55.2
1946	n.a.	−20.7	−18.2	−17.1
1947	n.a.	+ 0.7	+ 6.6	+13.2
1948	n.a.	+ 8.4	+ 8.9	+12.7
1949	n.a.	− 1.8	+ 1.0	+ 0.4
1950	n.a.	− 3.1	− 2.2	− 0.5
1951	n.a.	+ 3.5	+ 7.6	+16.2
1952	n.a.	− 4.0	[b]	− 1.0
1953	n.a.	− 9.4	− 5.3	− 6.5
1954	n.a.	− 3.1	− 0.2	− 8.5
1955	n.a.	− 4.2	− 2.7	− 0.1
1956	n.a.	+ 1.6	+ 4.5	+ 6.0
1957	n.a.	+ 1.6	+ 2.1	+ 4.7
1958	− 3.1	− 2.8	− 1.6	− 5.1
1959	−13.3	−12.4	−13.1	− 5.5
1960	0.2	+ 1.2	+ 0.8	+ 3.5
1961	− 3.5	− 3.9	− 2.3	− 2.7
1962	− 7.4	− 6.4	− 5.8	− 2.1
1963	− 4.7	− 6.3	− 4.0	− 1.2
1964	− 6.0	− 8.2	− 4.8	− 1.4
1965	− 1.1	− 3.4	− 2.7	+ 2.3
1966	− 3.7	− 2.3	− 3.3	+ 0.9
1967	− 8.8	− 9.9	− 1.5	− 7.5

Source: U.S. Bureau of the Budget.
n.a. Not available.
[a] Surpluses or deficits in the national income accounts for 1932–39 are for calendar years.
[b] Less than $50 million.

161

Table A-12. Net Federal Securities Outstanding, Net Interest on Federal Securities, and Private Debt in Relation to Gross National Product, 1916–67

(Dollar amounts in billions)

Year ending June 30	Net federal securities outstanding		Net interest on federal securities		Private debt	
	Amount	Percentage of GNP	Amount	Percentage of GNP	Amount	Percentage of GNP
1916	$ 1.2	2.4	$ .02	.04	$ 76.5	156
1917	2.9	4.5	.02	.04	82.4	128
1918	11.9	15.5	.19	.25	91.5	119
1919	25.0	29.3	.60	.71	97.2	114
1920	23.7	26.0	1.01	1.11	105.8	116
1921	23.4	32.2	.98	1.35	106.2	146
1922	22.0	30.2	.96	1.32	109.5	150
1923	21.8	25.5	1.04	1.21	116.3	136
1924	20.4	23.8	.91	1.06	123.0	143
1925	19.6	21.7	.85	.94	132.3	147
1926	18.6	19.2	.80	.82	138.9	143
1927	17.4	18.2	.75	.79	147.6	155
1928	16.5	17.0	.69	.71	156.1	161
1929	15.8	15.3	.68	.66	161.2	156
1930	14.6	16.1	.65	.72	160.4	177
1931	15.7	20.7	.60	.79	147.9	195
1932	17.1	29.5	.57	.99	136.7	236
1933	19.9	35.7	.65	1.16	127.5	229
1934	23.9	36.7	.71	1.09	125.1	192
1935	28.4	39.3	.77	1.06	124.2	172
1936	33.7	40.9	.70	.85	126.4	153
1937	35.0	38.7	.81	.90	126.7	140
1938	34.7	41.0	.85	1.00	123.1	145
1939	37.5	41.4	.84	.92	124.3	137
1940	39.0	39.1	.91	.91	128.6	129
1941	44.7	35.9	.95	.76	139.0	112
1942	63.7	40.4	1.01	.64	141.5	90
1943	119.3	62.3	1.50	.78	144.3	75
1944	168.6	80.3	2.20	1.04	144.8	69
1945	212.4	100.2	3.09	1.46	139.9	66
1946	217.0	104.1	4.10	1.97	154.1	74
1947	203.7	88.1	4.21	1.82	179.7	78
1948	195.2	75.8	4.20	1.63	200.9	78
1949	195.2	76.1	4.29	1.67	211.7	83

162

Table A-12—Continued

Year ending June 30	Net federal securities outstanding		Net interest on federal securities		Private debt	
	Amount	Percentage of GNP	Amount	Percentage of GNP	Amount	Percentage of GNP
1950	201.2	70.7	4.66	1.64	250.9	88
1951	194.2	59.1	4.43	1.35	282.2	86
1952	194.6	56.3	4.50	1.30	306.5	89
1953	196.4	53.9	4.99	1.37	329.8	90
1954	199.5	54.7	4.85	1.33	348.4	96
1955	203.0	51.0	4.87	1.22	402.5	101
1956	198.4	47.3	5.07	1.21	439.4	105
1957	196.4	44.5	5.25	1.19	467.8	106
1958	200.6	44.8	5.61	1.25	499.1	112
1959	208.3	43.1	5.50	1.14	547.4	113
1960	209.6	41.6	6.85	1.36	589.2	117
1961	209.9	40.4	6.71	1.29	634.6	122
1962	217.0	38.7	6.74	1.20	685.2	122
1963	220.6	37.4	7.38	1.25	747.6	127
1964	220.8	34.9	7.84	1.24	811.8	128
1965	220.5	32.2	8.15	1.19	890.0	130
1966	223.4	30.1	8.39	1.13	965.2	130
1967	225.5	28.3	9.13	1.16	1,030.3	131

Sources: Net federal securities outstanding is derived from Board of Governors of the Federal Reserve System, Banking and Monetary Statistics (FRS, 1943), pp. 509–10, 512, and Federal Reserve Bulletin, Vol. 36 (December 1950), p. 1658; The Budget in Brief, 1969 (1968), p. 71; U.S. Treasury Department, Treasury Bulletin, December 1967, p. 68.
Net interest on federal securities outstanding is derived from U.S. Bureau of the Census, Historical Statistics of the United States, Colonial Times to 1957 (1960), pp. 719–20; Economic Report of the President (1967), p. 283; Banking and Monetary Statistics, pp. 356, 512; Annual Report of the Secretary of the Treasury on the State of the Finances, Fiscal Year 1941 (1942), and Fiscal Year 1942 (1943); Treasury Bulletin, January 1950, p. 13, January 1952, p. 13, January 1954, p. 8, January 1956, p. 12, January 1965, p. 13, January 1966, p. 17, and January 1968, pp. 8, 16; Supplement to Banking and Monetary Statistics, Section 9: Federal Reserve Banks (FRS, 1965), p. 33; Federal Reserve Bulletin, Vol. 52 (February 1966), p. 270, Vol. 53 (February 1967), p. 308, and Vol. 54 (February 1968), p. A-88.
Private debt, 1916–28, is from Survey of Current Business, Vol. 33 (September 1953), p. 14; 1929–67, Economic Report of the President (1968), p. 277.
Gross national product, 1916–28, is from Raymond W. Goldsmith, A Study of Saving in the United States (Princeton University Press, 1956), Vol. 3, p. 427; 1929–63, U.S. Department of Commerce, The National Income and Product Accounts of the United States, 1929–1965 (1966), pp. 2–3; 1964–67, Economic Report of the President (1968), p. 209.

Table A-13. Ownership of Public Debt, 1939–67

(Par values in billions of dollars)[a]

Year[b]	Total public debt[c]	Debt held by U.S. government invest-ment accounts	Debt held by Federal Reserve banks	Privately held debt						
				Total	Commer-cial banks	Mutual savings banks and insurance com-panies	Other corpora-tions	State and local govern-ments	Individ-uals	Miscel-laneous
1939	47.6	6.5	2.5	38.6	15.9	9.4	2.2	0.4	10.1	0.7
1940	50.9	7.6	2.2	41.1	17.3	10.1	2.0	0.5	10.6	0.7
1941	64.3	9.5	2.3	52.5	21.4	11.9	4.0	0.7	13.6	0.9
1942	112.5	12.2	6.2	94.0	41.1	15.8	10.1	1.0	23.7	2.3
1943	170.1	16.9	11.5	141.6	59.9	21.2	16.4	2.1	37.6	4.4
1944	232.1	21.7	18.8	191.6	77.7	28.0	21.4	4.3	53.3	7.0
1945	278.7	27.0	24.3	227.4	90.8	34.7	22.2	6.5	64.1	9.1
1946	259.5	30.9	23.3	205.2	74.5	36.7	15.3	6.3	64.2	8.1
1947	257.0	34.4	22.6	200.1	68.7	35.9	14.1	7.3	65.7	8.4
1948	252.9	37.3	23.3	192.2	62.5	32.7	14.8	7.9	65.5	8.9
1949	257.2	39.4	18.9	198.9	66.8	31.5	16.8	8.1	66.3	9.4
1950	256.7	39.2	20.8	196.8	61.8	29.6	19.7	8.8	66.3	10.5
1951	259.5	42.3	23.8	193.4	61.6	26.3	20.7	9.6	64.6	10.6
1952	267.4	45.9	24.7	196.9	63.4	25.5	19.9	11.1	65.2	11.7
1953	275.2	48.3	25.9	201.0	63.7	25.1	21.5	12.7	64.8	13.2
1954	278.8	49.6	24.9	204.2	69.2	24.1	19.1	14.4	63.5	13.9
1955	280.8	51.7	24.8	204.3	62.0	23.1	23.2	15.4	65.0	15.6
1956	276.7	54.0	24.9	197.8	59.5	21.3	18.7	16.3	65.9	16.1
1957	275.0	55.2	24.2	195.5	59.5	20.2	17.7	16.6	64.9	16.6
1958	283.0	54.4	26.3	202.3	67.5	19.9	18.1	16.5	63.7	16.6
1959	290.9	53.7	26.6	210.6	60.3	19.5	21.4	18.0	69.4	22.1
1960	290.4	55.1	27.4	207.9	62.1	18.1	18.7	18.7	66.1	24.2
1961	296.5	54.5	28.9	213.1	67.2	17.5	18.5	19.0	65.9	25.0
1962	304.0	55.6	30.8	217.6	67.2	17.6	18.6	20.1	66.0	28.0
1963	310.1	58.0	33.6	218.5	64.3	17.1	18.7	21.1	68.2	29.2
1964	318.7	60.6	37.0	221.1	64.0	16.8	18.2	21.2	69.8	31.2
1965	321.4	61.9	40.8	218.7	60.8	15.8	15.8	22.9	72.1	31.4
1966	329.8	68.8	44.3	216.8	57.5	14.3	14.9	25.0	74.6	30.5
1967[d]	345.2	76.0	49.1	220.1	63.7	12.9	13.0	24.3	73.9	32.3

Source: *Economic Report of the President* (1968), p. 286.
[a] United States savings bonds, series A–F and J, are included at current redemption value.
[b] Values given for end of year.
[c] Gross public debt and guaranteed issues.
[d] Preliminary estimates.

Table A-14. Résumé and Lead Tables Used in Presidential Budget Messages, 1923-68

President and fiscal year		Budget concept used	
		In résumé table	In lead table (other than résumé)
Harding:	1923	Consolidated cash	Consolidated cash
	1924	New obligational authority (NOA) and consolidated cash	Consolidated cash
Coolidge:	1925	New obligational authority (NOA) and consolidated cash	Consolidated cash
	1926	New obligational authority (NOA) and consolidated cash	Consolidated cash
	1927	New obligational authority (NOA) and consolidated cash	Consolidated cash
	1928	New obligational authority (NOA) and consolidated cash	Consolidated cash
	1929	New obligational authority (NOA) and consolidated cash	Consolidated cash
	1930	New obligational authority (NOA) and consolidated cash	Consolidated cash
Hoover:	1931	Administrative budget and trust	NOA and consolidated cash
	1932	Administrative budget and trust	NOA and consolidated cash
	1933	Administrative budget and trust	Administrative budget and trust
	1934	Administrative budget and trust	NOA
Roosevelt:	1935	Administrative budget, trust, and NOA	Administrative budget
	1936	Administrative budget	Special relief acts
	1937	Administrative budget	Administrative budget
	1938	Administrative budget	Administrative budget
	1939	Administrative budget	Administrative budget
	1940	Administrative budget	Administrative budget
	1941	Administrative budget	Administrative budget
	1942	Administrative budget	Defense expenditures
	1943	None	None
	1944	Administrative budget and trust	War costs
	1945	Administrative budget and trust	War costs
	1946	Administrative budget and trust	War costs
Truman:	1947	Administrative budget and trust	Administrative budget
	1948	Administrative budget	Administrative budget
	1949	Administrative budget	Administrative budget
	1950	Administrative budget	Administrative budget
	1951	Administrative budget	Administrative budget
	1952	Administrative budget	Administrative budget
	1953	Administrative budget	Administrative budget
	1954	Administrative budget	Administrative budget and NOA
Eisenhower:	1955	Administrative budget	Administrative budget and NOA
	1956	Administrative budget and NOA	Administrative budget
	1957	Administrative budget and NOA	Administrative budget
	1958	Administrative budget and NOA	Administrative budget
	1959	Administrative budget and NOA	Administrative budget
	1960	Administrative budget, NOA, and consolidated cash	Administrative budget and NOA
	1961	Administrative budget, NOA, and consolidated cash	Administrative budget and NOA
	1962	Administrative budget, NOA, and consolidated cash	Administrative budget and NOA
Kennedy:	1963	Administrative budget, consolidated cash, NOA, and national income accounts (NIA)	Administrative budget
	1964	Administrative budget, consolidated cash, and NIA	Consolidated cash
Johnson:	1965	Administrative budget, consolidated cash, and NIA	Consolidated cash
	1966	Administrative budget, consolidated cash, and NIA	Administrative budget
	1967	Administrative budget, consolidated cash, and NIA	Consolidated cash
	1968	Administrative budget, consolidated cash, and NIA	Consolidated cash

Source: Ronald W. Johnson, "Evolution of Budget Concepts in the President's Message: 1923-1968," in President's Commission on Budget Concepts, *Staff Papers and Other Materials Reviewed by the President's Commission* (Government Printing Office, 1967), pp. 97-98.

Table A-15. Relation of Budget Authority to Outlays, Fiscal Year 1967

(In millions of dollars)

Type of budget authority	Amount
Budget authority requiring current action by Congress	
Enacted or transmitted herein:	
Appropriations	122,542[a]
Authorizations to spend debt receipts	7,742
Contract authorizations	5,110
Reappropriations and reauthorizations	38
Transmitted separately	
Appropriations	...
Contract authorizations	...
Total budget authority requiring current action by Congress	135,432
Budget authority becoming available without current action by Congress	
Appropriations	54,451[a]
Authorizations to spend debt receipts	1,264
Contract authorizations	2,952
Offsets in determining totals	
Interfund and intragovernmental transactions	−6,589
Applicable receipts from the public	−4,948
Total budget authority for the year	182,562
Unobligated balances and adjustments	
Unobligated balances	
Brought forward at start of year	121,228
Written off (rescinded, lapsed, and so on)	−1,169[b]
Carried forward at end of year	−134,490
Application of new authority to prior obligations	
Budget authority of year, obligated previously	−913
Budget authority of subsequent year, obligated currently	957
Net obligations incurred	168,175
Obligated balances	
Brought forward at start of year	69,387
Written off, less restorations, in expired accounts	−208[c]
Deficiency appropriations	83
Carried forward at end of year	−79,023
Outlays (expenditures and net lending)	158,414

MEMORANDUM

Outlays out of current authority	⎱ 158,414
Outlays out of prior authority	⎰
Total outlays	158,414

Source: Budget for Fiscal Year 1969, p. 58.
[a] Excludes appropriations to liquidate contract authorizations of $7,302 million.
[b] Includes adjustment of −$6 million for deficiencies in annual accounts.
[c] Includes adjustment of −$22 million for deficiencies in expired accounts.

Table A-16. Budget Authority and Outlays by Function, Fiscal Year 1967

(In millions of dollars)

Budget item	Budget authority	Outlays
Expenditure account		
National defense	75,276	70,095
International affairs and finance	4,336	4,110
Space research and technology	4,966	5,423
Agriculture and agricultural resources	4,318	3,156
Natural resources	3,262	2,113
Commerce and transportation	8,653	7,308
Housing and community development	1,503	577
Health, labor, and welfare	47,841	39,512
Education	4,430	3,602
Veterans' benefits and services	6,369	6,366
Interest	12,548	12,548
General government	2,463	2,452
Allowances for		
Civilian and military pay increase	...	...
Contingencies	...	...
Undistributed intragovernmental payments		
Government contributions for employee retirement	−1,735	−1,735
Interest received by trust funds	−2,287	−2,287
Total new obligational authority and expenditures	171,944	153,238
Loan account		
National defense	...	−3
International affairs and finance	779	540
Agriculture and agricultural resources	1,405	1,221
Natural resources	17	19
Commerce and transportation	938	138
Housing and community development	5,421	1,708
Health, labor, and welfare	570	572
Education	901	445
Veterans' benefits and services	590	532
General government	−3	2
Total loan authority and net lending	10,618	5,176
Total budget authority and outlays	182,562	158,414

Source: *Budget for Fiscal Year 1969*, p. 53.

Table A-17. Means of Financing, 1967, and Outstanding Debt, 1966 and 1967

(In millions of dollars)

Item	Amount	
	1966	1967
Budget financing		
Borrowing from the public		
Nonbank investors		−1,403
Commercial banks		405
Federal Reserve banks		4,549
Total borrowing from the public		3,551
Other means		
Seignorage on coins		813
Decrease (−) or increase in available cash and monetary assets		4,858
Increase or decrease (−) in liabilities for		
Checks outstanding (net of items in transit)		657
Deposit fund balances		−1,056
Total other means		5,272
Total budget financing		8,823
Outstanding debt at end of year		
Gross federal debt		
Public debt (issued by Treasury)	316,098	322,893
Agency debt (issued by agencies)	13,375	18,451
Total gross federal debt	329,473	341,343
Holdings by federally administered funds		
Public debt	63,697	70,537
Agency debt	167	1,647
Total holdings by federally administered funds	63,864	72,184
Net federal securities held by the public	265,609	269,160
Debt subject to public debt limitation		
Public debt	316,098	322,893
Portion of public debt issued to International Monetary Fund and international lending organizations	3,810	3,328
Portion of agency debt subject to limitation on public debt	462	512
Portion of public debt not subject to limitation (−)	266	262
Total debt subject to public debt limitation at end of year[a]	320,102	326,471

Source: *Budget for Fiscal Year 1969,* p. 61.

[a] The applicable public debt limitations are $328 billion from July 1, 1965; $330 billion from July 1, 1966; $336 billion from March 2, 1967; and $358 billion from July 1, 1968. The last limitation also covers certificates of participation issued in 1968; in addition, a temporary increase of $7 billion is provided from July 1, 1968, to June 29, 1969, and each year thereafter.

Bibliographical Notes

Chapter II. The Federal Budget: Concepts and Uses

Good general discussions and comparisons of the administrative, cash, and national income accounts budgets are provided in the following: "Budgets of the Federal Government," *Monthly Review of the Federal Reserve Bank of Saint Louis,* Vol. 44, No. 7 (July 1962), pp. 9–12; *Economic Report of the President* (Washington: Government Printing Office, 1962), pp. 77–78; "Federal Receipts and Expenditures—Alternative Measures," *Monthly Review of the Federal Reserve Bank of Kansas City,* August 1961, pp. 3–9; and Raymond Saulnier, "Three Federal Budget Concepts: Which Is Best?" *Vital Speeches of the Day,* Vol. 33, No. 13 (April 15, 1967), pp. 400–04.

For more detailed comparisons, see U.S. Congress, Joint Economic Committee, *The Federal Budget as an Economic Document,* 87 Cong. 1 sess. (Washington: Government Printing Office, 1962), Chap. 7; or the budget document itself for a particular year, for example, U.S. Bureau of the Budget, "Special Analysis A: Three Measures of Federal Financial Transactions," *The Budget of the United States Government, Fiscal Year Ending June 30, 1968* (Washington: Government Printing Office, 1967), pp. 394–402.

A more thorough explanation of the national income accounts and the federal national income budget may be found in U.S. Department of Commerce, Office of Business Economics, *National Income: A Supplement to the Survey of Current Business* (1954 ed.; Washington: Government Printing Office), Pts. 2 and 3; and in *U.S. Income and Output: A Supplement to the Survey of Current Business* (Washington: Government Printing Office, 1958), Chap. 2.

Good discussions of capital budgeting may be found in Maynard S.

Comiez, *A Capital Budget Statement for the U.S. Government* (Washington: Brookings Institution, 1966); Gerhard Colm, *The Federal Budget and the National Economy* (Washington: National Planning Association, 1955), pp. 94–100; Jesse Burkhead, *Government Budgeting* (New York: John Wiley, 1956), pp. 182–211; and Richard Goode and Eugene A. Birnbaum, "Government Capital Budgets," *International Monetary Fund Staff Papers,* Vol. 5 (February 1956), pp. 23–46.

There is considerable literature on the advantages and disadvantages of alternative budget concepts and suggested improvements. The *Report of the President's Commission on Budget Concepts* (Washington: Government Printing Office, 1967) is essential reading on this subject. A number of staff studies done for the commission are also valuable and appear in President's Commission on Budget Concepts, *Staff Papers and Other Materials Reviewed by the President's Commission* (Washington: Government Printing Office, 1967). Four particularly useful ones are: Ronald W. Johnson, "Evolution of Budget Concepts in the President's Message: 1923–1968," pp. 93–103; Stephen P. Taylor, "Alternative Concepts of Expenditure Timing," pp. 199–203; and two unsigned papers, "Coverage of the Budget," pp. 161–69, and "Netting and Grossing in the Federal Budget," pp. 245–61. The May 1963 issue of the *Review of Economics and Statistics* (Harvard University Press) was devoted to federal budget concepts and includes articles by Francis M. Bator, Samuel M. Cohn, Gerhard Colm and Peter Wagner, Otto Eckstein, Richard Goode, George Jaszi, Richard A. Musgrave, Carl Shoup, and Stephen Taylor, Helmut Wendel, and Daniel Brill. See also Chamber of Commerce of the United States of America, *Report of the Committee for Improving the Federal Budget* (Washington: the Chamber, 1962).

Chapter III. The Budget Process

The best general source of information on the budget process is Jesse Burkhead, *Government Budgeting* (New York: John Wiley, 1956), esp. Chaps. 4 and 10–14. There is a leaflet available from the U.S. Bureau of the Budget entitled "Preparation and Execution of the Federal Budget" (processed, 1962), which provides additional information on the federal budget cycle. Other good sources of general information are the following: U.S. Congress, Joint Economic Committee, "The Federal Budget Process," in *The Federal Budget as an Economic Document,* 87 Cong. 2 sess. (Washington: Government Printing Office, 1962), pp. 5–24; Arthur Smithies, *The Budgetary Process in the United States* (New York: McGraw-Hill, 1955); and Committee for Economic Development, *Control of Federal Government Expenditures* (New York: CED, 1955).

Sources of information on the planning-programming-budgeting system (PPBS) are given in U.S. Bureau of the Budget, "Program Analysis Techniques: A Selected Bibliography" (rev. ed., 1966). Its impact on the budget process is outlined in a Budget Bureau Bulletin, No. 68–2 (July 18, 1967).

Material on recent developments in federal budgeting is to be found in congressional hearings before the Subcommittee on Economic Statistics of the Joint Economic Committee, *The Federal Budget as an Economic Document,* 88 Cong. 1 sess. (Washington: Government Printing Office, 1963), pp. 149–212 (testimony by Charles L. Schultze, Samuel Cohn, and Carl Tiller, all of the U.S. Bureau of the Budget); U.S. Bureau of the Budget, "Improvements in Budget Presentation, 1947 to 1962," Staff Paper (August 1962): and Gerhard Colm, *The Federal Budget and the National Economy* (Washington: National Planning Association, 1955).

Chapter IV. The Record: Federal Spending and Taxes

The best single source of data on the record of federal spending and taxation is the budget document itself. Every issue contains historical tables for the cash, administrative, and national income accounts budgets. For example, the 1965 budget document contains a section of historical tables (pp. 453–63) on the three kinds of budgets. For less detailed data covering a longer period, see U.S. Bureau of the Census, *Historical Statistics of the United States, Colonial Times to 1957* (Washington: Government Printing Office, 1960), Series Y 205–714, pp. 709–30. Readable summaries of federal fiscal history are M. Slade Kendrick, *A Century and a Half of Federal Expenditures* (New York: National Bureau of Economic Research, 1955); Arnold M. Soloway, "The Growth of Government over the Past 50 Years: An Analytical Review," in U.S. Congress, Joint Economic Committee, *Federal Expenditure Policy for Economic Growth and Stability,* 85 Cong. 1 sess. (Washington: Government Printing Office, 1957); and Paul B. Trescott, "Some Historical Aspects of Federal Fiscal Policy," in *ibid.*

Details not found in any of these sources are sometimes available on request from the U.S. Bureau of the Budget.

Chapter V. Federal Budget Policy and the Economy

The relation between planned spending and GNP is discussed thoroughly in most basic economics textbooks; for example, see Charles L. Schultze, *National Income Analysis* (rev. ed.; Englewood Cliffs, N.J.: Prentice-Hall, 1964); Daniel M. Hamberg, *Principles of a Growing Economy* (New York: W. W. Norton, 1961), Chaps. 4–13; and Lloyd

Reynolds, *Economics: A General Introduction* (Homewood, Ill.: Richard D. Irwin, 1963), Chaps. 18–19.

The effects of tax or expenditure changes on planned spending, output, prices, and employment are also discussed in most of these same textbooks. See Schultze, *National Income Analysis,* Chap. 3, pp. 55–65; Hamberg, *Principles of a Growing Economy,* Chaps. 12 and 17; and Reynolds, *Economics,* Chap. 20. A relevant discussion may also be found in Otto Eckstein, *Public Finance* (2d ed.; Englewood Cliffs, N.J.: Prentice-Hall, 1967); and *Economic Report of the President* (Washington: Government Printing Office, 1963), pp. 45–52.

A discussion of the problems involved in using tax or expenditure changes to affect the economy may be found in Reynolds, *Economics,* Chap. 20; Eckstein, *Public Finance;* Hamberg, *Principles of a Growing Economy,* Chap. 17; and Wilfred Lewis, Jr., *Federal Fiscal Policy in the Postwar Recessions* (Washington: Brookings Institution, 1962), pp. 17–24.

The footnotes to this chapter give adequate references to works by the "money school" explaining their disagreement with the conventional analysis of the impact of budget policy and also to works discussing the problem of the mix of monetary and fiscal policy.

The concept of the budget line, the level of GNP, and the federal surplus or deficit is used in the *Economic Report of the President* (Washington: Government Printing Office, 1962), pp. 78–81. It goes back to a 1947 publication of the Committee for Economic Development, *Taxes and the Budget: A Program for Prosperity in a Free Economy,* and to statements by Charles L. Schultze, in *Current Economic Situation and Short-run Outlook,* Hearings before the Joint Economic Committee, 86 Cong. 2 sess. (Washington: Government Printing Office, 1961), pp. 120–22, and Herbert Stein, in *January 1961 Economic Report of the President and the Economic Situation and Outlook,* Hearings before the Joint Economic Committee, 87 Cong. 1 sess. (Washington: Government Printing Office, 1961), pp. 209 ff. See also Lewis, *Federal Fiscal Policy . . . ,* pp. 7–14.

The automatic fiscal stabilizers are discussed in the *Economic Report of the President* (1963), pp. 67–69, and Lewis, *Federal Fiscal Policy . . . ,* Chaps. 2 and 3.

Chapter VI. Fiscal Policy and the Budget Program

For general discussions of alternative budget policies, see Arthur Smithies, *The Budgetary Process in the United States* (New York: McGraw-Hill, 1955), pp. 437–69; Committee for Economic Development, *Taxes and the Budget: A Program for Prosperity in a Free Economy* (New York: CED, 1947); Committee for Economic Development, *Fiscal and Monetary Policy for High Employment* (New York: CED, 1962); Milton Friedman, "A Monetary and Fiscal Framework for Economic Stability," *American Economic Review,* June 1948, pp. 245–64; and Gunnar Myrdal, "Fiscal Policy in the Business Cycle," *American Economic Review,* Supplement, March 1939, pp. 183–93.

For a discussion of the full employment surplus as a measure of fiscal action, see Robert Solomon, "The Full Employment Budget Surplus as an Analytical Concept," *1962 Proceedings of the Business and Economic Statistics Section* [of the American Statistical Association] (Washington, n.d.), pp. 105–14. For an evaluation of the budget policy proposal of the Committee for Economic Development, see Walter W. Heller, "CED's Stabilizing Budget Policy after Ten Years," *American Economic Review,* September 1957, pp. 634–51.

Chapter VII. Fiscal Policy and the National Debt

For general discussions of the national debt, its history, its characteristics, and the economics of the debt, the following are recommended: Marshall A. Robinson, *The National Debt Ceiling: An Experiment in Fiscal Policy* (Washington: Brookings Institution, 1959); Ansel M. Sharp and Bernard F. Sliger, *Public Finance* (Homewood, Ill.: Dorsey Press, 1964), pp. 161–88; and the *Economic Report of the President* (Washington: Government Printing Office, 1963), pp. 78–83.

For more technical treatments of the question of the burden of the debt, and also other related issues, see James M. Buchanan, *Public Principles of Public Debt* (Homewood, Ill.: Richard D. Irwin, 1958); Alvin H. Hansen, "The Public Debt Reconsidered: A Review Article," *Review of Economics and Statistics,* November 1959, pp. 370–78; James E. Meade, "Is the National Debt a Burden?" *Oxford Economic Papers,* June 1958, pp. 163–83; Franco Modigliani, "Long-Run Implications of Alternative Fiscal Policies and the Burden of the National Debt," *Economic Journal,* December 1961, pp. 730–55; E. J. Mishan, "How To Make a Burden of the Public Debt," *Journal of Political Economy,* December 1963, pp. 529–42; Abba Lerner, "The Burden of Debt," *Review of Economics and Statistics,* May 1961, pp. 139–41; William G. Bowen, Richard G. Davis, and David H. Kopf, "The Public Debt: A Burden on Future Generations?" *American Economic Review,* September 1960, pp. 701–06; and Peter A. Diamond, "National Debt in a Neoclassical Growth Model," *American Economic Review,* December 1965, pp. 1126–50. Many of these articles are contained in a book edited by James

M. Ferguson, *Public Debt and Future Generations* (Chapel Hill: University of North Carolina Press, 1964).

Chapter VIII. Determining the Level of Federal Spending
For discussions of various proposals to share federal tax revenues with the states and localities and the criteria for allocating the financing of government programs at different levels of government, see George F. Break, *Intergovernmental Fiscal Relations in the United States* (Washington: Brookings Institution, 1967).

For a general discussion on the need for federal spending, the following are recommended: Francis M. Bator, *The Question of Government Spending* (New York: Harper, 1960); Robert L. Heilbroner and Peter L. Bernstein, *A Primer on Government Spending* (New York: Random House, 1963), Chaps. 1–4; Roland N. McKean, *Public Spending* (New York: McGraw-Hill, 1968); Gerhard Colm, "The Theory of Public Expenditures (1936)," in *Essays in Public Finance and Fiscal Policy* (New York: Oxford University Press, 1955), pp. 27–43; and Walter W. Heller, "Economics and the Applied Theory of Public Expenditures," in U.S. Congress, Joint Economic Committee, *Federal Expenditure Policy for Economic Growth and Stability,* 85 Cong. 1 sess. (Washington: Government Printing Office, 1957), pp. 98–107.

For a detailed discussion of cost-benefit and cost-effectiveness analysis as applied to federal spending, see A. R. Prest and Ralph Turvey, "Cost-Benefit Analysis: A Survey," *Economic Journal,* December 1965, pp. 683–735; Martin S. Feldstein, "Net Social Benefit Calculations and the Public Investment Decision," *Oxford Economic Papers,* March 1964; Stephen A. Marglin, "The Social Rate of Discount and the Optimal Rate of Investment," *Quarterly Journal of Economics,* February 1963, pp. 95–111; Charles J. Hitch, *Decision-Making for Defense* (Berkeley: University of California Press, 1965), pp. 43–58; Samuel B. Chase, Jr. (ed.), *Problems in Public Expenditure Analysis* (Washington: Brookings Institution, 1968); William M. Capron, "The Federal Budget: Program Budgeting, Program Analysis, and the Role of the Economist" (unpublished paper presented at Washington University in St. Louis, April 15, 1966); John F. Due, *Government Finance* (Homewood, Ill.: Richard D. Irwin, 1954), pp. 19–25; John V. Krutilla and Otto Eckstein, *Multiple Purpose River Development* (Baltimore: Johns Hopkins Press for Resources for the Future, Inc., 1958); Otto Eckstein, *Water-Resource Development: The Economics of Project Evaluation* (Cambridge: Harvard University Press, 1958); Charles J. Hitch and Ronald N. McKean, *The Economics of Defense in the Nuclear Age* (Cambridge:

Harvard University Press, 1960); and Robert Dorfman (ed.), *Measuring Benefits of Government Investments* (Washington: Brookings Institution, 1965). Rather complete bibliographies on the subject have been prepared by the U.S. Bureau of the Budget: "Program Analysis Techniques: A Selected Bibliography" (rev. ed., 1966), and "Supplement" (1967), both available (processed) from the Library of the Bureau of the Budget in Washington; and by Robert L. Chartrand and Dennis W. Brezina, Legislative Reference Service of the Library of Congress: "The Planning-Programming-Budgeting System: An Annotated Bibliography" (processed; Washington: Library of Congress, 1967).

Index

Accounting, in executive agencies, 41
Accrual accounting, in budget process, 7, 10, 12–13, 71n
Administrative budget, 2, 5, 9–11, 14–16, 18–19, 21, 34n, 42
Administrative lag, in fiscal policy, 89
Agency for International Development, 13
Agriculture, federal spending on, 40, 54, 57, 128, 139
Allotment, in budget process, 39
Analysis, in budget process, 25–30, 42–44, 134–36, 140, 144. *See also* Cost-benefit analysis
Annually balanced budget, 101–07
Apportionment, in budget process, 39, 41
Appropriations, 5, 9, 21, 29–30, 33; auditing of, 41–42; congressional action on, 36–38, 44–45; congressional committees on, 30, 32, 36–38, 44–46; coordination of decisions on, 46–47; defined, 34
Audit of accounts, 2, 41–42
Authority, budgetary, 5, 33–39, 89–90, 128
Automatic fiscal stabilizers, 91–93, 97, 100–01, 107
Automatic stabilizing budget, proposals for, 2, 102–07
Aviation, 137

Balance of payments, 2, 20, 62–63, 68–77, 81–89, 96–107
Balanced budget, 2, 80, 96, 99–107
Bankruptcy, public, 122–24
Banks, federal, 5, 12. *See also* Federal Reserve System
Barlow, Robin, 113n
Bator, Francis M., 142n
Bell, David E., 39n

Benefit-cost analyses. *See* Analysis, in budget process; Cost-benefit analysis
Berlin crisis, 61n, 105
Bollinger, Lynn L., 113n
Bonds, federal, 110–11, 118n
Borrowing, federal, 7–8, 17–20, 117, 123
Brazer, Harvey E., 113n
Break, George F., 113n
Budget, federal, 1–3; administrative, 5, 9–11, 14–16, 18–19, 21, 34n, 42; annually balanced, 2, 80, 96, 99–107; automatic fiscal stabilizers in, 91–93, 97, 100–01, 107; automatically stabilizing, 2, 102–07; capital, 5, 14, 17–21; concepts and uses of, 4–21; congressional consideration of (*see* Congress); consolidated cash, 2, 5, 9–12, 14–21, 42, 48; cyclically balanced, 104; divided, 15, 17–21; estimates for, 59, 60; improvements in, 42–43; national income accounts, 5, 9, 12–18, 21, 43, 71n; unified, 2, 5–18, 21. *See also* Budget policy; Budget process; Expenditures, federal; Revenues, federal; Taxes, federal
Budget Bureau. *See* Bureau of the Budget
Budget message, 22, 33, 42, 44
Budget policy, 22–23, 31, 48, 98–107, 143; effect on economy of, 62–97; and "formula flexibility" proposal, 106–07; impact on price level of, 62–63, 78, 84, 102; limitations of, 82–86, 113; and national debt, 108–24; and planned spending, 70–88
Budget process, 22–47; in agencies, 28–33, 37n, 39–41; analysis in, 25–30, 42–44, 134; apportionment and allotment of obligational authority during, 39, 41; and appropriations (*see* Ap-

177

178   Federal Budget Policy

propriations); and audit of accounts, 2, 41–42; and authorization, 5, 33–38, 89–90, 128; and execution of budget, 39–41; and executive preparation and submission of budget, 22–33, 43–44; fiscal side of, 31–32; improvements in, 42–45; review procedures in, 27–28, 32–33; timing of, 22–24, 33; and transmission of budget to Congress, 22, 33, 44; two-way flow of decisions in, 23–24; weaknesses in, 45–47, 103

Bureau of the Budget: apportionment of obligational authority by, 39, 41, 89; and budget process, 23–24, 26–28, 30–33, 38, 42; as one of "Troika" reporting to President, 44

Burkhead, Jesse M., 37n

Business, spending by, 63–65, 68, 70–73, 83–84, 86, 97. See also Private sector

Butters, J. Keith, 113n

Capital: movements of, 86; supply of, 118n, 120

Capital budget concept, 5, 15, 17–21

Cash budget, 48. See also Consolidated cash budget

Chase, Samuel B., Jr., 138n, 139n, 140n

Civil War, 49, 57

Comiez, Maynard S., 14n, 18

Commerce, Department of, 12, 89

Commercial audit, 41

Commission on Money and Credit, 90, 100

Committee for Economic Development (CED), budget proposals of, 2, 46–47, 90, 103–04

Commodity Credit Corporation, 7n, 13–14

Comprehensive audit, 41

Comptroller general, 41

Congress, U.S.: appropriations by, 36–38, 44–45; appropriations committees of, 30, 32, 36–38, 44–46; and auditing of federal expenditures, 41; budget committees of, 44–46; budget message to, 22, 33, 44; in budget process, role of, 1–2, 5, 30, 33–39, 44–45, 61–62, 89–90, 128; conference committees of, 38; discretionary fiscal action by, 93, 103, 105; and efficiency in expenditures, 129; and failure to coordinate expenditure and revenue decisions, 45–47; and income distribution, 140; tax legislation by, 99n, 106–07, 109, 111

Consolidated cash budget, 2, 5, 9–12, 14–21, 42, 48

Constitution, U.S., 128–29

Consumers: expenditures by, 12, 63–65, 68, 70–73, 117, 119–20; liquidity of, 83–84, 97

Copyright fees, 9

Cost-benefit analysis, as basis for budget decisions, 25–27, 29, 43, 46, 132–33, 136–39, 141, 143–44

Cost-effectiveness analysis, 134–36, 140, 144. See also Planning-programming-budgeting system

Costs, difficulty in measuring, 141

Council of Economic Advisers, 23, 31, 33, 44, 93–94, 109

Credit banks, federal, 5

Credit conditions, effect of, 71–72, 119

Cuban crisis, 105

Customs receipts, 57

Cyclically balanced budget, 104

Death taxes, 20, 140

Debt, national, 2–3, 9, 59, 108–24; as burden on future generations, 108–09, 117–21; defined, 109–13; in full employment setting, 118–21; growth of, 112–13, 123; interest on, 14, 29, 49, 51, 76n, 113–19, 123–28, 141; public concern over, 100, 107, 122–24; related to GNP, 113–15, 121–22; and social security, 111–12; in unemployment setting, 110, 117–18; in unified budget, 5, 8

Debt, private, 113, 115

Decentralization, 130–31, 136

Decision making, in budget process, 28–34, 44, 126, 134–38, 144

Defense, Department of, budget process in, 23n, 134

Defense, national: congressional authorization for, 34; cost-benefit analysis and, 144; effect of international situation on, 50, 61n; expenditures for, 99, 113, 125, 128–29, 131–35, 139, 141; federal responsibility for, 90, 142

Deficits: in balance of payments, 68–70; in different budget concepts, 5–8, 10, 17–19, 103–06; effect on economy of, 77n, 121–24; effect of tax rate or expenditure changes on, 78–80, 100; as measure of fiscal policy, 93–97, 121; public concern over, 91, 101–03, 107–09, 117–18; trends in, 48, 58–59

Deflation, 65

Departments, executive, budget process in, 28–33, 37n, 41